Speak
EATING FOR A HEALTHY LIFE
Live longer feel younger

Goals and Gains

You do not go from eating roadside junk to soyabean sprouts and scrambled egg whites overnight. To reach your ideal physique, incorporate small changes slowly rather than tackling a full-blown bodybuilding diet that is sure to be overwhelming. The most important factor that will help you succeed is consistency, both in training and nutrition. So make sure the diet you adopt is one you can maintain without feeling deprived or tolerating foods you dislike. To stick to a diet, you have to be able to live with it!

Staying healthy has become a major concern for all segments of the society today. We all aim at increasing 'longevity'. In our efforts to achieve it we are continually regulating calories and essential nutrients in our diet to fight menaces such as early ageing, obesity, heart problems, high blood pressure, diabetes, etc.

Checking calories in your diet is the cornerstone of *Eating for a Healthy Life* and is the essence of this book.

This book is essentially meant for calorie and health-conscious people.

Dr. Deepa Mehta is a researcher in Nutrition from Nagpur University. She has also coauthored the book, Speaking of: Diabetes and Diet, *published by Sterling Publishers under the Sterling Health Series. Her papers have been published in a number of journals.*

By the same author

Speaking of: Diabetes and Diet
(with *S.A. Vali*)

Published by
Sterling Publishers Private Limited

Speaking of
EATING FOR A HEALTHY LIFE
Live longer feel younger

Dr Deepa Mehta

A Sterling Paperback

STERLING PAPERBACKS
An imprint of
Sterling Publishers (P) Ltd.
A-59, Okhla Industrial Area, Phase-II,
New Delhi-110020.
Tel: 26387070, 26386209; Fax: 91-11-26383788
E-mail: sterlingpublishers@airtelmail.in
ghai@nde.vsnl.net.in
www.sterlingpublishers.com

Speaking of Eating for a Healthy Life

Revised Edition 2004
ISBN 978-81-207-1983-5
Reprint 2005, 2007, 2009

Printed and Published by Sterling Publishers Pvt. Ltd.,
New Delhi-110 020.

To my son, Shakti
and daughter, Pooja

PREFACE

As a guide, this book will help you to become a more active participant in your health care. Health is Wealth. Each chapter contains practical as well as essential information about the food items, their functions and how the relationship of your body, mind and food works. I have attempted to portray the present health consensus with regard to diet therapy and treatment modalities. I have tried to simplify this book by avoiding details of pathogenesis, complicated graphs and tables. Some tips are incorporated on the basis of my experience in the last 15 years. There is now an urgent need to put a brake on this escalating epidemic of malnutrition, which is a precursor of many diseases like diabetes, heart disease, hypertension, respiratory diseases, arthritis and spondylosis. This book is a small contribution towards this step.

This book is in seven units. Every unit of the book is complete in itself. Unit I deals with an introduction to food and its nutrients, with practical information and functions of each food group in a simple tabular form. It covers food which we eat but our body does not need, for example, caffeine, alcohol, fats and cholesterol, etc.

Unit II covers aspects of good health, to include basic food groups, the importance of meals and a variety of foods.

Unit III deals in detail about exercise.

Unit IV lists all the foods that can be interchanged, the calorific value remaining the same.

Unit V encompasses practical information regarding weight control and the logical substitution of high calorie foods with low calorie nutritious foods. This unit intends to assist the reader and his or her family members in implementing and carrying out the meal plan prescribed. It provides flexibility in planning a meal.

Unit VI deals with nutrition during infancy, childhood, adolescence, old age, pregnancy and lactation. It also covers special diets to meet abnormal physiological conditions like high blood pressure, diabetes, kidney problem, ulcers, heart problems and many others.

Unit VII is the ready-reckoner unit with a very handy and useful calorie-check reckoner, of almost all food groups.

There are almost 100 recipes mentioned in this book. Most of them use easily available ingredients, with the cooking directions clearly written.

With this kind of knowledge, comes a sense of self-confidence. Good health habits and regular medical care give your body the strength to withstand stress, and a healthy body will give your mind the will and resilience it needs to accomplish the work effectively and efficiently.

Dr Deepa Mehta

ACKNOWLEDGMENTS

The fact that words are indeed inadequate to express feelings of heartfelt gratitude is realized by me at this juncture. Yet, I want to try, in my most humble words to thank the personalities without whose excellent guidance and constant encouragement, this book would not have seen the light of the day.

I express my unflinching gratitude and loyalty to Dr Dhawan (AIIMS) for his kind co-operation. I gratefully acknowledge Dr Sharad Pendsey, Diabetologist and his staff for his scholarly advice and valuable comments. They have provided friendly guidance in abundance with fruitful academic interaction.

Also I would especially like to thank Mr Man Singh and Mr Baldev Sharma for their generous help in completion of the work.

I am grateful to Mr SK Ghai and Sterling Publishers for publishing this book.

CONTENTS

UNIT I

EAT RIGHT — THE EASY WAY

WHAT IS FOOD MADE UP OF?

A number of basic elements combine to form the food we eat. These elements in food are called *nutrients* and include proteins, fats, carbohydrates, minerals, vitamins, trace elements and water. Eating nutritious food in a balanced combination so that the body gets all the nutrients it needs is the best way to achieve that golden aim — good health. Remember, you may be well-fed but still not well-nourished.

You need to learn about what you are giving your body and what your body needs. Generally, a balanced diet is the best route to good nutrition. Before you can balance the food in your diet, you have to understand how food affects your body. What does the body need to function successfully? Why should certain foods be eliminated from your diet?

Learning all about food can be quite complicated but there's no need to go into elaborate details. What you need to know, can be explained simply, all that is required is an understanding of why our bodies need nutrients, how these nutrients are used and what life-sustaining elements are there in our food. Once a person is aware of these 'unknowns' and how these affect his health, he will be much more careful about what he eats.

A glass of milk ... , a slice of bread ... , how much iron is recommended for pregnant women ... ? Ready answers to questions like these are helpful while planning a balanced diet. Food values of various foodstuffs can be easily referred to in the tables in this book. Also there are balanced diet charts so that you do not have to count nutrients, weigh food or calculate vitamin and mineral content every time you prepare a meal. It has all been done for you. The purpose is to help you learn what is in the food you eat.

Food That We Need

Food is essential for normal functioning and survival. The food that we eat is used as fuel for energy, but no single foodstuff provides all the nutrients needed by the body. This is where *balancing a diet* comes in.

Proteins

Known as the muscle-building nutrient, it is broken down into individual amino acids during digestion and absorption. The amino acids are then taken up by the body for various jobs like manufacturing tissues and enzymes needed for metabolism. Everyone needs protein, but how much should you eat to shuttle enough of those amino acids to your muscles?

Basically, if you are eating a balanced diet (15–20 per cent of your daily calories should come from proteins) you should get enough to support muscle growth (aim for 0.8 gms per kilogram of body weight). If you are a very active weight trainer, athlete or heavy worker which means you have larger muscles that are working harder, you may benefit from a 20 per cent increase in daily protein. In other words, while an average man weighing 70 kg can stay healthy with about 56 grams of protein daily, an athlete, a weight trainer or heavy worker will need about 66 to 70 gms daily. Exceeding this amount over a long period could lead to kidney problems and an abnormal metabolic condition called ketosis. The following chart is to familiarise you with rich sources of protein and their appropriate measures.

Sources of Proteins

Vegetarian Foods with Protein	Non-Vegetarian Foods with Protein
Cottage Cheese (Paneer) 	Fish 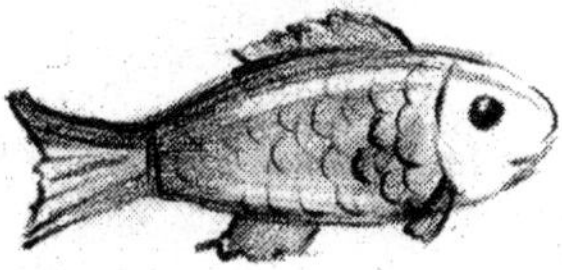
Peas 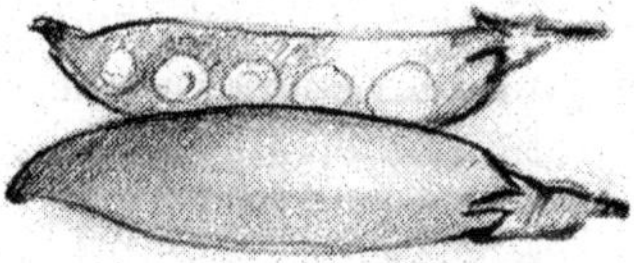	Eggs 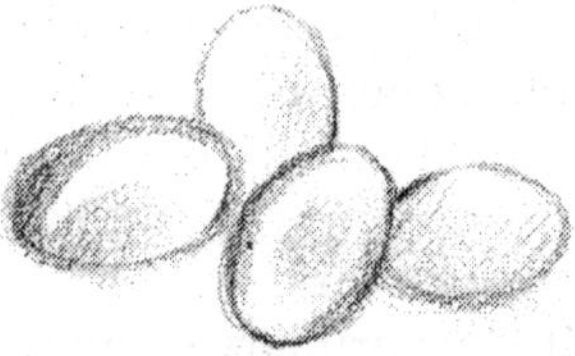
Cheese 	Meat 
Pulses 	

Table 1.1 : Protein Content in Common Foods

Food	*Average serving in gms*	*Proteins in gms*
Milk (whole)	240	9
Meat (lean)	85	22
Cheese (cottage)	28	5
Egg	1	6
Soyabean	60	4
Dry non-fat milk	17.5	6.5
Beans	128	7.5
Peas, green	80	4

Carbohydrates

If you lead an active lifestyle, your body needs fuel in the form of carbohydrates to function optimally. How many carbohydrates you should eat each day depends on your total energy intake, size and health status, as well as the duration, intensity and type of exercise you do.

If your primary exercise is strength training, at least half of your food should be rich in carbohydrates, whether you are trying to gain or lose weight. Aiming for 50%–60% of your daily calories from carbohydrates should be enough. Endurance exercise such as long-distance running, depletes liver and muscle glycogen, the body's stored form of carbohydrates, which is why competitive athletes often need extra carbohydrates.

If you spend serious hours in the gym, ignore the countless diet books that recommend minimal carbohydrates and maximum proteins. Drastically reducing your carbohydrates intake may cause your body to absorb protein from your muscles and use amino acids to fuel your workouts, and protein is too precious to waste on filling up your energy tank.

Carbohydrates include oatmeal, whole-grain foods, vegetables, beans and lentils. Complex carbohydrates like these should form the bulk of your diet.

Glycemic Index of Food

Over the past few years, grouping carbohydrates according to glycemic index has become increasingly popular. High glycemic

Sources of Carbohydrates

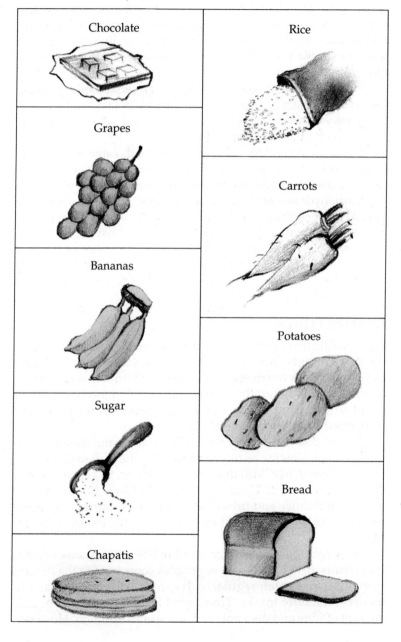

Chocolate

Grapes

Bananas

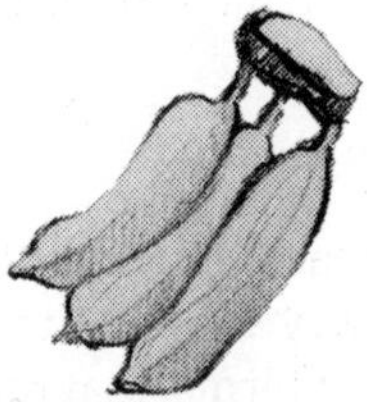

Sugar

Chapatis

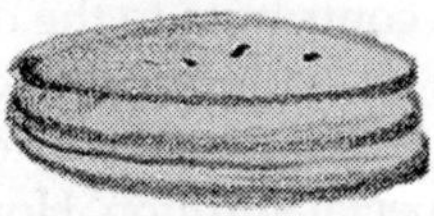

Rice

Carrots

Potatoes

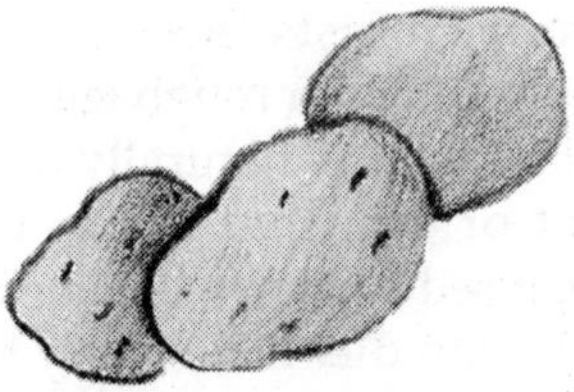

Bread

index foods are less desirable, the theory being that they cause a rapid rise in insulin and blood glucose, possibly having negative consequences on health and body-weight in some individuals. Foods lower on the glycemic index are generally believed to be more desirable for their slower and sustained effect on blood glucose and insulin.

However, since many so-called high-glycemic foods belong to the nutritious variety, eg bread, rice, carrots, potato and banana—I suggest you simply ignore this controversial system of ranking foods, except if you are a diabetic.

Just keep in mind that high-glycemic foods eaten with protein or fat, moderate the insulin/glucose response, so glycemic index rating matter more only when carbohydrates are eaten alone.

Carbohydrates are your labour force, so make them work for you. When possible, choose oatmeal, yams, whole-grain breads and cereals, pasta, potatoes and rice over flimsy white bread, processed foods like biscuits and crackers, and other snacks like pizza and burgers. First preference should be fruits and vegetables to pack your body with nutrients and help build a foundation of health.

Dietary Fibres

Fibre in nutrition has been an area of increasing interest for study by nutritionists the world over. Dietary fibre, unavailable carbohydrates or roughage are the different terms, that refer to the total amount of naturally occurring material in foods, mainly of plant origin, that is not digested. Dietary fibre is widely recognised to have a beneficial effect.

Indian diet has a fairly high fibre content and therefore the dietary requirements as recommended by the Indian Council of Medical Research (ICMR) do appear excessive. An average Indian diet contains about 25–35 gms of crude fibre. Today, due to western influence and urbanisation the consumption of highly refined food has increased, thereby reducing the intake of dietary fibre.

However, excellent sources of fibre like wholegrains, cereals, fresh fruits, dried fruits and vegetables contribute to the dietary fibre intake, if eaten regularly. It can be added to the diet to increase the fibre intake. Traditional Indian diet has adequate amount of fibre and does not need any special addition. However, with rapid urbanisation and industrialisation, diet is being replaced by tinned foods, fast foods and so on and hence the need to supplement fibres, arises. For practical purposes daily fibre intake of 20 to 30 gms is adequate. Too much fibre in the diet can cause gaseous distention, diarrhoea and bloating.

However, it is not good to increase fibre intake suddenly. A sudden increase makes the patient feel distended with abdominal discomfort and increased flatulence, especially if the initial fibre intake was low. Some patients like to take their additional fibre in the form of bran, but on the whole it is better to take a balanced high fibre diet that they can enjoy for the rest of their lives.

Food Rich in Fibre

Food products commonly available in India and rich in fibre are as follows:

- *Millet Preparations:* cooked as cereals or homemade snack
- Red beans
- Sprouts of pulses, gram or beans
- *Amongst Vegetables:* cluster beans (*guar*), curry leaves, drumstick or lotus stem
- Guava and pomegranate are the fruits with the highest fibre content
- Certain items commonly used as condiments enrich the food preparations with fibre, eg green chillies, cardamom, coriander, etc.

The indigenous system of medicine in India employs some plant preparations that are rich in fibre content, eg *fenugreek (methi), neem, jamun, karela (bitter gourd), psyllium (Isabgol).*

In diet planning, the most beneficial metabolic profile is produced by a high carbohydrate low-fat diet. These high carbohydrate diets for diabetics are effective only when relatively large amounts of unrefined carbohydrates and fibre are included, such as legumes, unprocessed vegetables and fruits.

Delicious Ways to Add Fibre

- Use of whole wheat and gram in the ratio of 3:1 for chapatis is better than plain wheat chapatis.
- Mix equal portions of rice and whole pulses for idli, dosa and khichri.
- Select wholewheat bread or soya bread instead of white bread.

- Drink 6–8 glasses of fluid daily to help your body to use fibre effectively.
- Include more of uncooked vegetables and sprouted beans in your salad.

A diabetic who is a vegetarian and likes wholesome and coarse food with natural fibre, mixed proteins and restricted fat of unsaturated nature, will lead a healthy life.

Following is a list of food items classified according to fibre content – high, medium and fibre free:

Table 1.2 : Food Sources of Fibre

High fibre Foods	*Medium fibre foods*	*Fibre-free foods*
Wheat bran, whole wheat, whole wheat flour, broken wheat (*dalia*), unpolished rice, corn, oats, ragi, *bajra and jowar*, whole and split pulses, beans and peas, banana, papaya, guava, plums, grapes, dried fruits, dark green and leafy, vegetables, drumsticks, lady's finger, fenugreek seeds	Brown bread, cornflakes, green vegetables, brinjal, carrot, beetroot, potatoes, onion, radish turnip, apples, orange, sweet lime	Sugar, egg, butter, oil, cheese, cottage cheese

Dietary Fibre Content of Some Indian Foods

Foodstuff	*Dietary Fibre*
I. *Cereals and Millets*	(gms) %
Rice	7.6
Wheat	17.6
Sorghum	14.3
Bajra	20.3
Ragi	18.6
II. *Pulses and Legumes*	
Green gram (whole)	15.2
Green gram (split)	13.5
Black gram (split)	14.3

	Foodstuff	*Dietary Fibre* (gms) %
	Red gram (split)	14.3
	Bengal gram (whole)	14.1
	Bengal gram (split and unhusked)	26.6
III.	***Nuts and Oilseeds***	
	Groundnut	6.1
	Coconut (dry)	8.9
IV.	***Roots and Tubers***	
	Sweet potato	7.3
	Potato	4.0
	Yam	5.3
	Carrots	7.0
V.	***Fruits***	
	Banana	2.5
	Mango	2.3
VI.	***Vegetables***	
	Amaranth	3.4
	Spinach	5.0
	Brinjal	2.0
	Ridgegourd	5.7
	Snakegourd	1.8
	Bottlegourd	2.8
	Pumpkin	0.5
	Beans and peas	0.7

Source: *B S Narsinga Rao, Nutrition Foundation of India Bulletin 9: (4), 1988.*
Note: *Fibre Content indicated is per 100 gm of foodstuff.*

Fats

When it comes to calories, all fats are the same — equally undesirable. Containing 9 calories per gram, fat has more than twice the calories of carbohydrates and proteins. A high-fat diet increases the risk of obesity and its complications (diabetes, hypertension and certain cancers). It is another reason to be judicious with all fats, even with the more desirable ones such as olive and peanut oil.

Remember that fat is only a part of the equation. To reduce your risk of heart disease, hypertension and certain cancers, it is just as important to eat lots of fruits and vegetables and whole grains, which provide vitamins and fibre.

Regular exercise is as vital as a sound diet in the fight against heart disease, stroke, obesity, hypertension, diabetes and certain cancers. With a balanced programme, you can win that fight — and enjoy life while you are at it.

Facing the Fats

If your motto is 'fat is bad', here is a shocking news: Some fats are turning out to be very healthy. So healthy, in fact, that you probably need more!

How Fats Affect Your Health?

Nearly all the fats in our diet are in the form of triglycerides. Because triglycerides in food are so large, they cannot be absorbed directly into the blood. Instead, the pancreas and intestines produce enzymes that break down the dietary fat into individual fatty acids that are absorbed into the bloodstream.

In general, fats come from animal sources such as meat and dairy products; oils come from vegetable products. But the situation is more complex: animal fats are high in saturated fatty acids. In broad terms, saturated fatty acids raise blood cholesterol levels and increase the risk of heart disease, while unsaturated fats do not.

Fats and oils are essential components of human diet and 20% to 25% of the total calories should come from them. In a 2000 calorie diet this amounts to 40–50 gms of oil per day.

- Polyunsaturated fats are less atherogenic than monounsaturated and saturated fats.
- Vegetable oils have high content of polyunsaturated fats while saturated fats are present mainly in fats of animal origin, eg egg yolk, fatty meat, milk creams, butter and ghee.
- Essential fatty acids like linoleic acid n-6 (Omega-6) and linolenic acid n-3 (Omega-3) cannot be synthesized by the human body. Hence they must be taken through diet, and therefore, they are called essential fatty acids. They play an important role in lipid physiology and they protect against atherosclerosis by lowering cholesterol levels, regulating clotting mechanisms and by maintaining the stability of vascular endothelial cells.

Sources of Fats

Clarified Butter (*Ghee*) 	Groundnuts (Peanuts) 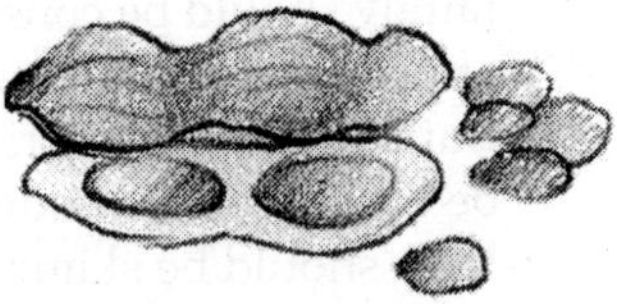
Oil 	Almonds 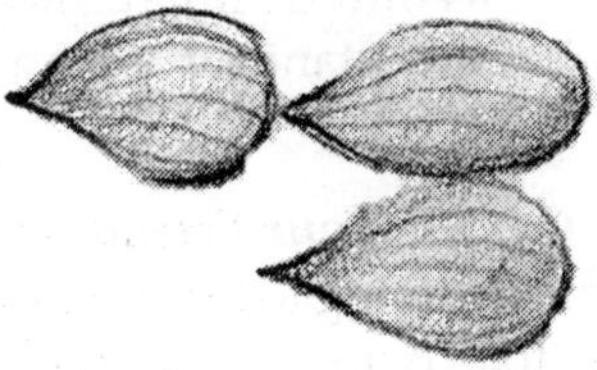
Butter 	Potato Chips 

- Omega 6 (linoleic acid) is present in vegetable oils, cereals, pulses, etc. Omega 3 (linolenic acid) is present in marine products like fish. The ratio of Omega 6 to Omega 3 fatty acids in diet should be 5:1. Hence fish has been rated a very healthy non-vegetarian food that protects against heart diseases.
- Cereals, pulses, meat, tubers also contain some amount of fat and it is called as invisible fat.

Important Advice

- Vegetable oils: How much oil is important? Which oil should one go for? There is no need to buy special cooking oil, the traditionally used vegetable oil in the family should be consumed. The quantity of oil should be approximately 20 mg/day (4 teaspoons).
- Butter and ghee are rich in saturated fats and they should be consumed in moderation, 10 gms (2 teaspoons) a day. Milk should be skimmed before consumption.
- Hydrogenated Fats (Vanaspati Ghee) should be avoided.
- Non-vegetarian food like egg yolk, organ meats should be avoided. Meat should be lean (after removing the subcutaneous skin) and should be cooked in less amount of oil.

Fat Can Be Your Friend or Foe, Depending on Your Goals

If you are trying to lose body-fat, watch out for dietary fat: It packs more than twice the calories per gram – 9 cal/gms as carbohydrate or protein 4 cal/gms. But if you are struggling to gain mass, increasing your fat intake is an easy way to increase your calorie intake. Just do it by eating nuts, seeds and vegetable oils rather than slathering butter over everything.

Cholesterol

Cholesterol is not a fatty acid but a sterol, a waxy substance with a complex, ringlike structure. Cholesterol is present only in animal tissues; all foods derived from plants have no cholesterol.

For all their notoriety, fats and cholesterol are crucial for good health. Cholesterol is present in human cell membranes and is the backbone of the steroid and sex hormones manufactured by the body. Fatty acids are also incorporated into cell membranes; each type of fatty acid affects cell function differently. In addition, fatty acids are stored as triglycerides in the body's adipose tissue, which provides insulation, protects and cushions vital organs, and functions as the body's principle energy depot.

The body can produce all the cholesterol it needs; that is why strict vegetarians stay healthy even though their diet contains no cholesterol. The body can also make most of the fatty acids it needs simply by converting one fat into another. But there are two exceptions: because the body cannot produce linoleic acid (an Omega–6) or alpha-linolenic acid (an Omega–3), eating these two polyunsaturated fatty acids is essential for health, though only small amounts are needed.

Healthy individuals limit their fat intake to about 20% of their total daily calories, sometimes even lower, which falls below the general guidelines of keeping fat under 30% of your calorie intake. Be careful not to drop your fat intake too low; this macronutrient is vital in cushioning and lubricating your body's cells and also has an exercise–related function.

Very intense exercise like bodybuilding relies more on carbohydrates for fuel; low to moderate aerobic exercise relies more on fat. The longer you do aerobic exercise, the more your body will tap circulating fatty acids and stored body fat, since the body can store only a limited amount of glycogen — the stored form of glucose comes from carbohydrate — in the muscles and the liver.

Total diet of meats should be 250 gms = 20-30 gm of Cholesterol. Cholesterol rich foods are egg yolk, organ meats like brain, kidney, liver and milk products like butter and ghee.

Various ways of decreasing cholesterol and saturated fat in the diet are:

- The use of the unsaturated oils should be restricted to ½ kg per person per month.
- Use skimmed or low-fat milk and milk products.
- Instead of butter use cottage cheese or curd.
- Decrease the use of red meat. Instead use fish or chicken.
- Bake, broil, roast, boil or steam your foods instead of frying them in oil.

Types of Cholesterol

The Good Cholesterol (HDL):This cholesterol is a waxy substance made by the liver, essentially to maintain cell walls and work as a double-edged sword. Good cholesterol or High Density Lipoprotein (HDL) cholesterol keeps the arteries clear by mopping up the junk deposited by its bad cousins i.e. LDL. They usually fight a losing battle.

The Bad Cholesterol (LDL):This is a cousin of good cholesterol called Low Density Lipoprotein (LDL), which clings to the walls of blood vessels and apart from damaging cell linings, gathers other substances to form plaque, a hard, thick substance that narrows the arteries considerably.

The Ugly One (Triglycerides): This one is a malevolent customer obtained from foods like butter. Known as Triglyceride (TG), it actually performs a good role, providing instant energy. Excess TG, however, tends to get stored as body fat in the blood and assists LDL in its destructive ways. Indians are genetically inclined to high levels of LDL and TG.

The Terrible One Lipoprotein LP (a):The nastiest is called Lipoprotein LP (a) that thickens blood flow. It is 10 times more potent than LDL. The problem is that genetically, Indians have one of the highest levels of LP (a), which combined with high LDL and TG levels causes various heart problems.

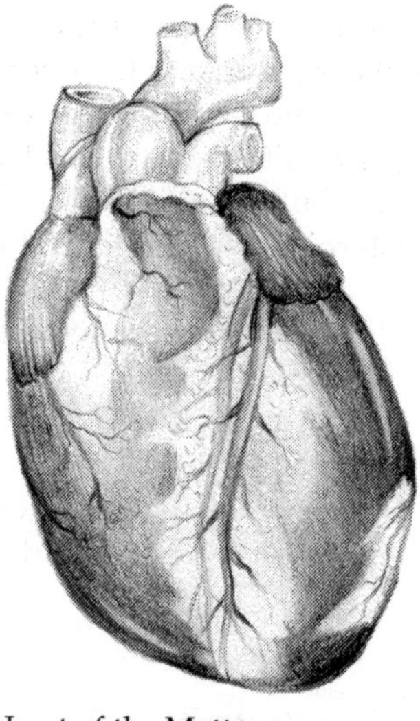

Heart of the Matter

The Good

The Bad

The Ugly

The Terrible

Types of Cholesterol

The Good Cholesterol: High Density Lipoprotein (HDL)
The Bad Cholesterol: Low Density Lipoprotein (LDL)
The Ugly one: Triglyceride (TG)
The Terrible and the Nastiest: Lipoprotein LP (a)

The heart pumps fresh blood to all parts of the body. Muscles derive energy from oxygen dissolved in blood flowing through the coronary arteries. Keeping the main highway free from obstacles for transportation of blood is a daily war.

The Fats You Eat

Saturated Fats

Animal	Vegetable
Dairy fats	Coconut oil
Meat and poultry	Cocoa butter
Tallow	Palm oil
Lard	Palm kernel oil

Cholesterol

Dairy Products
Egg yolks
Meat (especially organ meats, fatty and prime cuts)
Shellfish (especially shrimp)

Monounsaturated Fats

Omega–9

Olive oil
Mustard oil
Peanut oil
Rapeseed oil

Polyunsaturated Fats

Trans–Fatty Acids	Omega–6
Margarine	Corn oil
Fried foods	Safflower oil
Commercially packed Goods	Sunflower oil
Various snacks	Soyabean oil
Cottonseed oil	Sesame oil

Omega–3

Fish	Vegetables
Mackerel	Mustard oil
Tuna	Walnuts
Salmon	Flaxseed
Sardines	Rapeseed
Others	Wheat germ
	Soya seed

Table 1.3: Fat in gms per 135 calories

Polyunsaturated Fats			
- Safflower oil	15 gm	- Sunflower oil	15 gm
- Corn oil	15 gm	- Soyabean oil	15 gm
- Cottonseed oil	15 gm	- Sesame (til) oil	15 gm
- Rice-bran oil	15 gm	- Groundnut oil	15 gm
Saturated Fats (To be avoided)			
- Margarine	20 gm	- Coconut oil	15 gm
- Clarified butter	15 gm	- Clarified butter	20 gm
- Mayonnaise	20 gm	- Cream, heavy	40 gm

Some Simple Ways to Reduce Fat in Your Diet

(a) Remember that the saturated fats are the ones you do not need. The polyunsaturated fats are fine. Watch your intake of oils and butter. When you do use oil, use only the polyunsaturated kind.

(b) Try not to eat red meat, it is unbelievably high in fat.

(c) Always remember to remove the skin of a chicken. A whole fried chicken has about 2,000 calories but if you remove the skin, you are left with just about 1,000 calories, which is quite a difference!

(d) Read the fat content in the food chart Table 1.4 and remember that high fat content foods can be substituted by foods containing less fat. For instance, the difference between the amount of fat in whole milk and that in non-fat milk is considerable.

Fats and Cholesterol

The following chart contains a list of foods with their fat and cholesterol content. Read it carefully—you may be in for a surprise! For example, did you know that skimmed milk curd has less than half the fat content (and therefore less than half the cholesterol) as compared to whole milk curd?

Table 1.4 : Fats and Cholesterol

Food	*Amount*	*Fat (in grams)*	*Cholesterol (mg)**
Butter	4 oz/110 gm	92.0	260
Cake, sponge	4 oz/110 gm	30.0	147
Cheese, processed	4 oz/110 gm	28.0	99
Cottage cheese	4 oz/110 gm	4.5	14
Chicken, roast	4 oz/110 gm	4.5	83
Custard, egg	4 oz/110 gm	6.8	113
Poached egg	4 oz/110 gm	11.7	544
Scrambled egg	4 oz/110 gm	22.7	464
Hard, boiled egg	4 oz/110 gm	0.0	04
Crab	4 oz/110 gm	5.8	113
Codfish, steamed	4 oz/110 gm	1.0	68
Herring, grilled	4 oz/110 gm	14.7	90
Lobster	4 oz/110 gm	3.8	170
Dairy ice-cream	4 oz/110 gm	7.4	23
Macaroni	4 oz/110 gm	2.2	0
Margarine	4 oz/110 gm	91.0	0
Mayonnaise	4 oz/110 gm	89.0	294
Milk, skimmed	4 oz/110 gm	1.0	2.2
Milk, whole	4 oz/110 gm	4.8	15.8
Olive oil	4 oz/110 gm	113.0	Minute traces
Peanut oil	4 oz/110 gm	113.0	Minute traces
Sunflower oil	4 oz/110 gm	113.0	trace
Pudding, bread & butter	4 oz/110 gm	8.8	113
Whole wheat bread	4 oz/110 gm	0.3	0

**mgs = milligrams*

Analysing Cholesterol

Actually the test carried out in a fasting state estimates the levels of serum cholesterol, HDL cholesterol and triglycerides only. The other levels are derived by using Friedewald formula.

eg, $\text{VLDL (mg/dl)} = \frac{\text{Triglyceride}}{5}$

LDL cholesterol (mg/dl)

$$= \text{Serum cholesterol} - \text{HDL cholesterol} - \frac{\text{Triglyceride}}{5}$$

and the various ratios like Cholesterol/HDL, Cholesterol/LDL, LDL/HDL are calculated by dividing one value by the other. End result is a full page report on lipid profile with multiple numerical values. One needs to only concentrate on three values namely cholesterol, triglyceride and HDL and see whether HDL is low or cholesterol and triglycerides are raised.

Management strategy depends upon which abnormality exists in the given patient.

	Good	Acceptable	Poor
Serum Cholesterol mg/dl	<200	200 – 240	>240
HDL Cholesterol mg/dl	>45	35 – 45	<35
Triglycerides	<350	150 – 200	>350

< less

> more

Best Insurance Against Disease – Prevention

After initial assessment of lipid levels, counselling on general lifestyle modification should be given including abstinence from smoking, encouragement of regular aerobic exercises and dietary advice. The preventive measures are amazingly simple and they do work. The key is to keep your body healthy.

Dietary Advice

It will generally include reducing total fat intake, particularly reduction of saturated fats, limiting cholesterol intake and increasing fruit, vegetable and complex carbohydrate intake and reducing body weight whenever appropriate.

Alcohol Intake

Although small quantities of alcohol, eg. 45–50 ml/day is said to increase HDL cholesterol, larger quantities of alcohol intake leads to hypertriglyceridemia, abstinence from alcohol normalises or reduces triglyceride levels. If you enjoy alcohol, drink responsibly and moderately.

Walking

Walking is an excellent aerobic activity for cardiovascular conditioning and is also known to increase HDL cholesterol and reduce total cholesterol and triglycerides. Jogging, climbing stairs, dancing, racquet sports, cycling and calisthenics will also help.

Glycemic Control

Good control of diabetes brings down raised triglyceride values to a normal range dramatically and it also helps in increasing the levels of HDL cholesterol.

Drug Therapy

The use of lipid lowering drugs should be considered only if conservative approach fails. In patients with established CHD (Coronary Heart Disease), aggressive approach to lipid reduction is recommended.

Do not overlook effective precautions just because they seem so obvious. Follow the advice that Shakespeare gives in Henry IV, part I: "Out of this nettle, danger, we pluck this flower safely."

Water

How much of your body is made up of water? Actually, more than half—about 60% of you is plain old H_2O. It lubricates your cells, regulates body temperature and affects your ability to exercise, among many other functions. And people with more muscle mass contain even more water, since muscles and organs contain more water than body fat stores do. If you are active, you need more than the baseline of eight glasses a day, particularly before, during and after exercise. You will know you are well-hydrated if your urine is colourless/pale yellow and you are using the restroom frequently. Most importantly, do not wait until you are thirsty to drink water!

Minerals

Minerals are of vital importance and are found in most of the foods we eat, particularly in vegetables, meat and fish. Minerals needed by the body can be classified into two groups. One group is the *macro-minerals* which are needed in large amounts. These include calcium, potassium, phosphorus, magnesium, sodium, sulphur and chlorides. The *micro-minerals* which we need only in minute amounts and which are easily obtained from a normal balanced diet is the second group. These include iron, zinc, manganese, copper, iodine and others.

Sources of Minerals

Apples 	Milk 
Bread 	Eggs 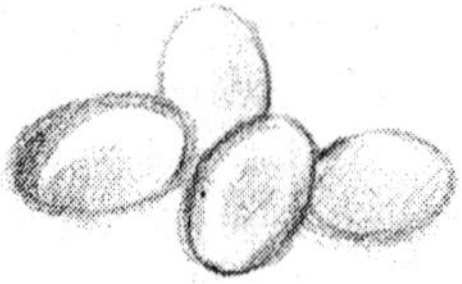
Carrots 	Bananas 

Minerals also keep you free from diseases. They also help build up your teeth, bones and blood. You need them in very small quantities.

Table 1.5: Food Sources of Minerals

Mineral	*Source*	*Needed for*
Calcium	Cottage cheese, non-fat or low-fat dairy products, cream, whole milk, cheese, green leafy vegetables, sardines, tinned salmon (with bones), citrus fruits, dried beans, almonds	Bones and teeth, muscle contraction, blood clotting and cell membranes
Phosphorus	Processed cheese, non-fat or low-fat dairy products, fish, poultry, meat, cream, whole milk, cheese, eggs, nuts, dried beans	Bones and teeth, formation of cell membranes and enzymes
Magnesium	Nuts, whole grains, green leafy vegetables, fish	Bones and making proteins
Iron	Meat, eggs, green leafy vegetables, whole grains, dried fruit, dried beans	Supply oxygen to cells, proteins and enzymes
Zinc	Meat, fish, eggs, chicken	Makes up enzymes
Iodine	Iodised salt, fish	Functioning of thyroid, reproduction
Potassium	Dried fruits, orange, bananas, meat, peanut butter (no oil) dried beans, potatoes, vegetables	Muscle contraction, release of energy from proteins, fats, and carbohydrates, nervous system

Vitamins

Vitamins are substances needed in small quantities but they are indispensable. They perform specific vital functions and are essential components in any diet. *Vitamin supplements* are a subject of continuing controversy in the health world. It is often said that vitamins provide added energy and vitality. However, the truth is that while the deficiency of vitamins may cause illness, an excess of them definitely does not make one healthier. The chart below shows how vitamins affect our health.

Sources of Vitamins

Oranges

Chapatis

Tomatoes

Milk

Eggs

Carrot

Lemons

Vitamins keep you healthy by helping your body fight diseases. They also help other body organs and parts like eyes, nerves, gums, skin, etc work properly. Just a small quantity is needed but you must have them everyday. Otherwise you can be very, very sick. Vitamins are called by different names – Vitamin A, Vitamin B, Vitamin C, Vitamin D, Vitamin E, etc.

Supplements Help

A few choice supplements may help you reach your goals more quickly. Here is a rundown of the basics.

Protein Supplements

You can usually get all your protein from food without difficulty. However, if you are short of cooking skills or are time crunched then supplements are a convenient though expensive alternative. Look for a formula that your body easily tolerates and that tastes good. To up the calories, have the shake with a snack or even drink it with a full meal.

Vitamins and Mineral Supplements

A multivitamin can act as an insurance policy if you are not getting enough nutrients from food. Taking extra antioxidants like vitamins C and E may also be beneficial. But do not go overboard on micronutrient megadoses — some can be toxic in excess amounts (like Vitamin A). Women may want to consider calcium supplements, particularly if they are on a low-calorie diet.

How the Vitamins Affect Your Health

Vitamin A **Promotes vision and healthy skin**

Sources: Liver, eggs, milk, butter, cheese, yogurt, carrots and other yellow vegetables and green leafy vegetables.

Vitamin B **Promotes healthy skin, especially around the mouth, nose and eyes. Promotes a well-functioning nervous system**

Sources : Milk, wholegrain cereals and breads (wheat germ, bran), meat, poultry, fish and vegetables like beans, peas, etc.

Vitamin C **Promotes the healing of wounds, and strong teeth and bones**

Sources: Citrus fruits and juices, tomatoes, beans, sprouts, green leafy vegetables and strawberries.

Vitamin D **Promotes strong bones and teeth**

Sources : Milk, eggs, meat, cheese, butter, sunlight on bare skin, fish-liver oils, canned tuna and sardines.

Vitamin E	**Assists vitamins A and C, certain fats and the red blood cells in performing their specified roles in the body** Sources : Whole grains, whole cereals, vegetable oils, eggs, liver, fruits, vegetables, seeds, nuts, wheat germ and beans.
Vitamin F and K	**Is needed in the blood-clotting mechanism** Sources: Green plants such as spinach, cabbage, and kale; also produced by the bacteria normally inhabiting the intestines.

Food That We Do Not Need

I certainly do not advocate a life of total abstinence. But there is a smart way to live that does not include eating or drinking substances that will harm you. Once you know how damaging cholesterol, sodium present in common salt, sugar, caffeine and alcohol can be, it will be a lot easier for you to minimise and control their intake.

Fats and Cholesterol

As mentioned earlier, foods with high content of fat and cholesterol can be dangerous and have an adverse effect on health. So do not indulge in high cholesterol and fat rich food.

Sugar

The sweetness of sugar may turn sour when you comprehend the harm it can do to your body. Natural sugar found in fruits is not harmful. But refined sugar is nothing but empty calories. It can add on fat to your body because you eat more calories than your body can burn off. Sugar damages the teeth, can cause serious diseases like diabetes and hypoglycemia and may disturb the entire body system.

By now you must have got the point that refined sugar has no nutritional qualities. But the question is, how to stop eating it? That is difficult but not an impossible task, because sugar is found in almost everything we eat.

The solution to the control of sugar intake is twofold. Firstly, try to cut down on the sugar intake itself by moderation in the consumption of sugar. For example, do not add sugar to beverages and drinks. Develop the habit of eating fruits instead of sweets as snacks and watch your energy levels shoot up!

Secondly, try to avoid or even eliminate foods that are high in sugar content, from your diet. This does not mean that you completely deny yourself sweet food but if you decide to allow yourself the pleasure of eating sweets now and then, an occasional adjustment of a low calorie meal with sugar-rich food, is a sensible way to cater to that sweet tooth.

Therefore, minimising sugar in your diet is not all that difficult.

Sodium in Common Salt

Sodium is a necessary mineral, but too much of it is harmful. Most of us consume far too much, forgetting that an excessive intake of sodium has been the cause of high blood pressure, strokes, kidney diseases and many other problems.

Therefore, we need to cut down on sodium by not adding salt to cooked food, because many of the foods we eat already have an enormous sodium content. Also ensure that at least once a week, you do not consume salt at all. Observe that day as a 'salt fast day'.

When reading the chart on the 'Sodium Content of Foods' remember that foods high in sodium, if taken in smaller quantities, may not be that harmful. If you try to limit your intake you would remain ahead in the game of staying healthy. Here are some tips:

a) Do not add salt to your food.

b) Do not keep a saltshaker on your table. If the shaker is not there when you want it, you may not want it after all.

c) Use herbs and spices like garlic, onion or lemon juice for added flavour instead of salt.

Table 1.6 : Sodium Content of Common Foods

Food	*Amount (in gms)*	*Sodium (in mg)*
Baked beans, tinned	110	545
Bread		
crumbs	110	861
white	110	612
whole wheat	110	612
Butter, salted	110	986

Cheese		
cottage	110	610
processed	110	1,542
Cornflakes	110	1,315
Pizza	110	385
Salmon, tinned	110	646
Salmon, smoked	110	2,131
Soup, powder	110	6,350
Soup, tinned		
cream of chicken	110	521
cream of mushroom	110	532
tomato	110	521
Soya sauce	110	1,621
Spaghetti, tinned	110	567
Sweetcorn, tinned	110	351

Caffeine

Drinking coffee in moderation is fine, but as a matter of habit, caffeine is an addictive drug and like all drugs has its drawbacks. Scientists have found a correlation between drinking a lot of coffee and developing a high level of cholesterol, which, of course, can lead to heart disease.

Table 1.7 : Caffeine in Common Drinks

Drink	*Amount*	*Caffeine (in mg)*
Instant coffee	170 ml	79
Brewed coffee	170 ml	120–180
Decaffeinated	170 ml	3
Tea (tea bag)	170 ml	35–50
Iced tea (homemade, lemon, no sugar)	170 ml	35
Coca-Cola	300 ml bottle	35–65

Fast Foods

As the following table 1.8 shows, most fast foods lack vitamins, mainly vitamins A and C, but are high in sodium, sugar and saturated fats. So, pause a while if the urge to gorge on hamburgers, chips and pizzas seizes you. Just think — a meal at a fast food restaurant is worth almost 3500 calories! What one can do, however, is to limit the food one eats at these restaurants and balance them with nutritional meals at other times of the day.

Table 1.8: Contents of Fast Foods

Food	*Calories*	*Fat (in grams)*	*Sodium (in mg)*
Chips	211	10.6	112
Fish sandwich	440	24.0	707
Fried chicken	830	46.0	535
Fried shrimp	381	24.4	537
Hamburger	290	13.0	525
Cheeseburger	350	17.0	724
Milk-shake			
chocolate	324	8.4	329
vanilla	324	7.8	250
Pizza (3 slices)	450	16.0	1,140

Alcohol

Alcohol furnishes no carbohydrate, protein or fat and is not at all healthy as a nutrient. Nevertheless alcohol is packed with calories, 1 gm of alcohol yields 7 calories. Another thing one must remember is that with alcohol people smoke a lot which is injurious to health, and eat lot of fried food which further increases the calorie intake.

Drinking Formula

There are many medical reports published in authentic medical journals, highlighting the importance of moderate alcohol consumption and its relation to reducing the risk of coronary heart disease. Moderate alcohol consumption has been said to increase HDL cholesterol levels and thereby reducing the risk of CAD. Those patients who cannot sleep without alcohol should be recommended to drink alcohol in moderation. The alcohol consumption should be restricted to about 5% of the total calories in a day. Generally, this is equivalent to about 45 ml of whisky or related alcoholic drinks.

Alcoholic Drink	*Measure*	*Calories*
Beer	1 glass (250 ml)	120
Gin	1 peg (60 ml)	162
Rum	1 peg (60 ml)	162
Whisky	1 peg (60 ml)	162
Sweet wine	100 (ml)	150

"I never drink alcohol; I only have wine." Is this you?

Most adults do not realize that there is as much alcohol in 125 ml of wine or 300 ml of beer as there is in 40 ml of hard liquor. And that means you could be sabotaging your health when you think you are toasting to it. You have read about studies showing that people who drink alcohol have less heart disease and stroke. But the headlines usually miss this critical point: Health benefits from alcohol happen at moderate intake levels only — that is one drink a day for women, two for men. Once you go over that line, the risks start adding up fast.

Just four or five drinks within 24 hours — common at social events — increases the short-term risk of a stroke almost five times in those who are at a high risk.

UNIT II

A GLANCE AT GOOD HEALTH

INTRODUCTION

Health consciousness has been in full swing in our country for over two decades now. Today you see morning walkers and joggers; health clubs, gymnasiums and weight control clinics springing up everywhere. This health revolution has changed our outlook, even our language has significantly changed. Earlier, we were somewhat concerned only about calories but now we are aware of carbohydrates, fat, proteins, cholesterol content, fibre content and similar other details. Today, people are concerned not only about the food they eat but also how best to use them so as to maintain health.

Good health means much more than just 'not being sick'. It is within the control of each one of us to lead not only a 'not sick' life but to attain the best health possible so as to remain physically and mentally active.

Today, the emphasis is on preventive medicine, instead of allowing oneself to fall ill. Preventive medicine centres on two premises. The first is an alliance with nutrition and food, eating habits, awareness of foods and preparation of special diets for preventive health.

The other area that preventive medicine encompasses is that of 'physical fitness'. Some form of exercise is absolutely essential for both physical and mental well-being.

Balanced food and *fitness* are the twin pivots of good health. If you are healthy, you look good. Good health has enormous benefits. If you are eating well, relaxing right and exercising enough, you look trim, feel good and look attractive. Good health means more than just the well-being of the body, it is also the positive condition of one's mind and spirit which must function as smoothly as one's body.

Nothing is more beautiful than a human being in excellent health. Eating well and keeping your body fit are the basics, but a number of extra measures can be taken to give you the best physical fitness possible.

Principles of Good Health

Forming Healthy Eating Habits

It is never too late to learn how to eat in a healthy manner. It is important to learn about and form good eating habits. Eat in moderation, avoid excesses and be vigilant about foods to be restricted, the quantity which should be eaten and when.

Know About What You Are Eating

When you have even a small amount of basic scientific knowledge about the relationship between food and your body, you can learn how to eat properly and healthily. You need to educate yourself about the food you eat, learn what food you need for good nutrition and how to avoid gaining unnecessary and unhealthy weight.

Moderation and Balance as the Cornerstone of a Successful Diet

Complete denial is not necessary. As long as you understand that moderation is the key to healthy eating, you can eat your favourite dishes, but do remember to compensate any lack of nutrition or overeating in other meals. The idea is to take the best care of your body so that you will look and feel the way you want.

Physical Fitness

Some forms of exercise are absolutely essential for physical well-being and for mental health as well. Walking, swimming, cycling, aerobics or playing your favourite game regularly will keep you fit. Above all, enjoy whatever exercise you do.

Dieting to Lose and Maintain Weight

Diet is what you eat. It is not abstinence from eating. It should be merely an understanding of how to eat well, whether it is to lose weight or to maintain it.

Be Flexible

Remember to be flexible enough in your diet plans or in your exercises as a practical approach to life. Forcing yourself through rigidity in food or exercise which may not be convenient sometimes, does not work well.

Keep Abreast of Information on Nutrition

Books, magazines, TV, radio or even a talk with a doctor or dietitian always give you an update on the latest research or suggestions on nutrition.

Adhere to Dietary Goals

Make right exercising and right eating a permanent way of life, by sticking to the 'no' and 'yes' rules which you make for yourself.

Eat Natural Food

Natural food tastes wonderful and preserves an appreciable amount of vitamins and minerals. Red and green salads, fresh from the garden and wholegrain bread are much more nutritious and healthy than overcooked food.

Keep off the Lethal Five

Avoid excessive fat, refined sugar, salt, coffee and alcohol.

Basic Food Groups

A simple and convenient way to study the different common foods is to group them in several classes according to the nutrients they supply most abundantly. There are five well-known food groups, each group comprising foods similar in the general chemical make-up which contribute the same types of nutrients to the diet.

Good nutrition also means eating a variety of foods from different food groups. No single food group supplies all the essential nutrients to maintain good health. But a food plan that includes a suggested number of servings from different food groups, furnishes the nutrients that should be in an adequate diet.

Table 2.1 : Five Food Group Systems and Their Roles

Food Group	Role in the Diet
I. ***Cereals and Their Products***	
Bread, whole wheat, wheat flour, cornmeal, rice, noodles, spaghetti, macaroni. Other cereals (maize, jowar, bajra, oats, etc)	They are inexpensive sources of energy and proteins. Whole grain carries more iron and vitamins and has an appreciable amount of roughage.
II. ***Pulses and Legumes***	
Bengal gram, black gram, green gram, red gram, lentils (whole as well as husked dals) cowpeas, kidney beans (*rajma*), soybeans, beans, etc and fibre.	They provide energy, proteins, invisible fat, vitamin-B_1, vitamin-B_2, folic acid, calcium and iron
III. ***Fruit and Vegetable Group***	
a) *Fruit and Vegetables rich in Vitamin C*	
Oranges, grapefruit, lime, lemons, strawberries, sweet lime, guavas, tomatoes, cabbage, sprouts, turnips, etc	They are rich in vitamin C.
b) *Fruit and Vegetables rich in vitamin A*	
Mangoes, papayas, carrots, pumpkin, sweet potatoes, yam, spinach, amaranth, coriander, fenugreek, etc.	They are rich in iron, vitamin A and folic acid.
IV. ***Milk and Meat Products***	
a) *Milk Products*	
Whole milk, skimmed milk, milk powder, evaporated milk, condensed milk, buttermilk, curd, cheese ice-cream, iced milk, etc.	They are valuable source of proteins, minerals especially calcium.
b) *Meat Products*	
Beef, lamb, pork, organ meat such as heart, liver, kidney, brain; poultry such as chicken, goose, turkey, fish, etc.	They are rich in proteins and minerals.
V. ***Fats and Sugar***	
Fats	
Butter, ghee, hydrogenated oil; cooking oil like groundnut, mustard, coconut, etc.	They provide energy, fat and essential fatty acids.
Sugar	
Sugar, jaggery, etc.	They provide energy.

Assessment of Good Health

Obese people should try their best to control their diet. Failure to lose weight through diet and exercises is sometimes due to lack of self-control.

Once a person gains enough weight to enter the realm of obesity, say an extra 25 pounds as an adult, the body's normal fat regulation processes stop working properly. The body's metabolism erroneously stores more and more calories as fat, and fat begets more fat. An obese person in this situation, finds no success with dieting and faces both society's condemnation and the health consequences of obesity.

Some important tips for extending your healthy years are:

- Eating right amount of nutritious food
- Maintaining one's blood pressure and weights
- Decreasing alcohol consumption as it decreases life expectancy

How to Maintain a Healthy Life

Aging cannot be avoided but can definitely be delayed.

Check Your Habits

1. If you smoke, stop it.
2. If overweight, reduce and try to maintain that weight.
3. Maintain your blood pressure.
4. Exercise regularly.
5. Keep your blood cholesterol and triglyceride levels within a normal range.
6. Keep your blood sugars under control.
7. Reduce stress and be happy.

Stop Smoking

Did you know that cigarette smoking is known to adversely affect nearly every system or function in the human body. Smoking has been linked to diseases and disorders ranging from diabetes to cataracts and from cancer to impotence. Nicotine narrows and restricts blood vessels and has other such dangerous effects. The single most important thing that you can do is stop smoking and thereby stop the damage caused by nicotine.

Lose Weight if Overweight

Being overweight tends to increase your blood sugar, blood pressure and blood fat levels. Even a modest 5–10 kg weight loss will improve your condition. To lose weight, avoid crash weight loss programs. Emphasis should be on low-fat eating and more exercise. These will also help keep your blood sugar and blood fat levels within a healthy range.

Keep Blood Pressure in Control

High blood pressure increases the risk of stroke. Have your blood pressure tested at least twice a year. If your blood pressure is over 130/80, lose weight. This is a lower target than for people who do not have diabetes. Follow a low salt meal plan. Exercise more. And ask your doctor about medications to lower blood pressure.

Exercise More

Exercise keeps your heart healthy and helps keep blood sugar and blood fat levels in control.

Consult an exercise expert to start a sensible exercise program. Be sure to check with your doctor before beginning an exercise program. Also be sure to ask if there are types of exercise you should not do because of other complications you may have due to diabetes.

Define a set schedule for exercise. You will be surprised how much better you feel!

Keep Your Fats and Cholesterol in Control

High levels of blood fats, including cholesterol, increase the risk of heart disease. With diabetes, you are more likely to have high blood fat levels. There is proof now that lowering levels of so-called bad cholesterol (LDL cholesterol) in persons with diabetes greatly lowers the risk of a heart attack.

Your level of HDL (so-called good cholesterol) should be at least 42 mg%. Your level of LDL (so-called bad cholesterol) should be under 100 mg%. Your triglyceride level (another bad fat) should be under 200 mg%

To reach these goals, follow a low-fat, high fibre, lower calorie meal plan. Weight loss decreases blood fat levels. See a dietitian for help. Exercise lowers levels of bad fats and increases levels of good fats. Blood fat lowering medications may be needed if your cholesterol levels do not respond to these treatments.

Keep Blood Sugar in Check

Monitor your blood sugar regularly. Learn to check blood sugar yourself. Know how to adjust your diet, exercise, medication, if blood sugars are unusually high (above 180 mg/dl) or unusually low (below 70 mg/dl).

HbAlc is a blood test, which tells how well your blood sugar has been controlled over the past two months or so. If it is over 7.5% ask for help with your treatment plan. (*For detailed information on diabetes refer to the book* Speaking of : Diabetes and Diet *by the same publisher.*)

Chart Your Diabetes Care

To prevent heart or coronary disease you should have the following tests and discuss with your doctor what to do, if the results are not normal.

Every 3–6 months

- HbAlc test
- Blood
- Weight check

Every Year

- Blood fats check (total cholesterol, LDL and HDL cholesterol and triglycerides) if previous levels were normal.
- Urine check for albumin to assess the functioning of the kidneys. Consult a dietitian or exercise expert for help in losing weight, starting an exercise programme or improving blood sugar control as needed.

How Much Should We Eat?

A balanced diet meets all the nutritional needs of a person. There is no ideal diet since each diet is a matter of individual requirement. The various nutrients needed by the body have been discussed. Here, the principles of nutrition will be translated into the selection of an adequate diet in the right proportion.

The recommended dietary allowance is a basic guideline for good nutrition. It shows the average requirements for different age-groups, depending on occupational activity.

Classification of Activities Based on Occupation

Sedentary

Male: Teachers, tailors, barbers, executives, shoemakers, retired personnel, landlord, peons, etc.

Female: Teachers, tailors, housewives, nurses, executives, etc.

Moderate

Male: Fishermen, potters, goldsmiths, agricultural labourers, carpenters, masons, electricians, fitters, turners, welders, industrial labourers, drivers, priests, postmen, weavers, etc.

Female: Maidservants, basket-makers, weavers, beedi-makers, agricultural labourers, etc.

Heavy

Male: Stonecutters, blacksmiths, mine workers, woodcutters, sportsmen, athletes, soldiers, salesmen, gangmen, rickshaw pullers, coolies, etc.

Female: Stonecutters, players, athletes, dancers, saleswomen, etc.

Table 2.2 : Recommended Dietary Allowances for Indians

Group	*Particulars*	*Net Energy cal*	*Protein gm*	*Fat gm*	*Calcium gm*	*Iron gm*
Man	Sedentary worker	2350				
	Moderate worker	2700	60	15	400	28
	Heavy worker	3200				
Woman	Sedentary worker	1800				
	Moderate worker	2100	50	15	400	30
	Heavy worker	2450				
	Pregnant woman	+300	+15	25	1000	38
	Lactation					
	0-6 months	+ 550	+ 25	35	1000	38
	6-12 months	+ 400	+ 18			
Infant	0-6 months	118/kg	2.05/kg	-	500	-
	6-12 months	108/kg	1.65/kg			
Child	1-3 yrs	1125	23	20	400	12
	4-6 yrs	1600	31	20	400	18
	7-9 yrs	1925	41	15	400	25
Boy	10-12 yrs	2150	53	15	600	28
Girl	10-12 yrs	1950	55	15	600	20
Boy	13-15 yrs	2400	71	15	600	42
Girl	13-15 yrs	2050	67	15	600	28
Boy	16-18 yrs	2600	79	15	500	50
Girl	16-18 yrs	2050	65	15	500	30

Guide to the Homemaker

The task of planning a nutritious meal centres around the essential nutrients included in optimal amounts. In addition to this, attention must be paid to the palatability, cultural appropriateness and feasibility of the diet. People do not eat solely for nutrition. Social, cultural and psychological factors are to be kept in mind while planning an acceptable diet.

Basic Guidelines for Good Food

Good food and good health can go together in everyone's daily life.

a) Choose much of what you eat from foods in their raw or natural state. Eat raw vegetables in salads, fruits, grains like unpolished rice and whole wheat bread and lean cuts of meat and fresh fish. This way you will get all the essential nutrients.

b) Good health begins with the basic ingredient of choosing fresh food full of goodness and vitamins. Do not ruin it with poor preparation and bad health habits. Firstly, that means being careful about storing the food you bring home. A bowl of fruit left uncovered loses vitamins in the light and warmth of the room. After 3 days at normal room temperature, fruits and vegetables may have lost up to 70 per cent of their vitamins A, B and D. Store food carefully in a cool dark food cupboard or in a refrigerator.

c) Meat and poultry are perishable foods. They should be kept in the refrigerator for best conservation and a longer storage life.

d) Do not waste good vitamins by throwing away carrot tops, beetroot tops, cabbage hearts or other greens. They make delicious vegetable dishes when steamed for a few moments with a few fresh herbs and a little butter. The not-so-perfect bits are good for soups.

e) Get into the habit of steaming vegetables instead of boiling them. Steaming keeps all the vitamins and minerals intact instead of being drained away in the water thrown away. Do not overcook. Vegetables taste so much better when they are slightly crisp and chewy instead of a messy water-sodden lump. Almost all recipes which call for boiling can be adapted to steaming. This includes fish and meat.

f) Pots and Pans! Nonstick pans are a great boon to a careful cook since it means food can be fried with the minimum of fat. Nonstick pans can replace the classic frying in most recipes.

g) Decrease the amount of fat, salt and sugar in your diet. While lean meats do contain hidden fat, you can cut off all visible fat from meat and use less butter. Replace sweet desserts with fresh fruits.

h) Alcohol uses up B-complex vitamins and other important nutrients from your body. A glass of wine often relaxes tension and stimulates the palate but too much alcohol has harmful effects.

i) Freezers! Freezing is a boon. No matter what sort of diet the family is used to, freezing preserves fresh food more quickly than any other form of storage. It also keeps vitamins in their original form as far as possible. Meat, vegetables, bread, desserts, almost everything can be prepared for freezing. And it is convenient too.

Planning Meals

Do not skip meals, plan them. If any meal is omitted or neglected, there is too much nutritional load put on the remaining meals and snacks in a day's intake. For example, if breakfast is omitted, the intake of nutrients for the day is inadequate or the food intake is concentrated later in the day instead of being divided over twenty-four hours. At times, snacks which are mainly 'empty' calories, fast foods and drinks comprise the entire day's food, if there is only 'snacking' and no 'mealing'.

Skipping breakfast is more common in cities than in rural areas and is not related to income. Eating breakfast has been found essential for maximum efficiency — both physical and mental. Avoiding breakfast results in decreased output and decreased mental alertness.

Sometimes five or six meals are preferable to the usual three. Milk or raw salad allowances could be taken in between meals in this case.

For weight reduction, the following suggestions will be helpful:

a) It should be emphasised that a low-calorie diet of about 1000 cal/day is advisable to achieve effective and steady weight reduction. This intake can however be doubled after achieving the desired weight for its maintenance.

b) Remember that you will not always be on the same low-calorie bland diet, but will eventually enjoy most foods with slight restrictions.

c) Instructions on calorie balancing when the stage of weight maintenance is reached, will permit most people to include their favourite foods in the diet.

d) Very rapid weight loss should be discouraged. Crash dieting to lose 2–3 kg per week, gradually results in a loss of will power and eventually, in breaking the diet. It is better to lose weight gradually so as to maintain the desired weight.

e) Meals should be balanced and properly spaced. It is important to have breakfast and to avoid the temptation to snack between meals. As breakfast usually follows a 12–15 hours period of starvation (the word 'breakfast' means to 'break a fast'), it is important to provide energy to the body early in the morning.

f) Diet education and induction of new healthy eating habits is very essential to keep yourself slim and fit. Seek professional help if necessary as continuous counselling and encouragement will go a long way in keeping you motivated to stay mentally and physically fit.

Variety of Dishes

Sprouts, soyabeans and its products, mushroom, green leafy vegetables, *'missi atta'** and higher fibre foods are highly nutritious. They are less commonly used because of our ignorance about their importance. A glance at their nutritive values will reveal how indispensable they are.

Sprouts

All beans /legumes can be sprouted. Sprouts are:

a) Low in calories — 30 cal / 100 gm
b) Low in carbohydrates — 6 gm / 100 gm
c) Protein content is about 3 gm / 100 gm
d) High dietary fibre
e) Appreciable amount of vitamins A, B and C

* 'missi atta' – Wheat and Bengal gram flour

How to Sprout Legumes

Soak legumes overnight. Drain and cover with a thin cloth and keep sprinkling water 2 to 3 times a day for 2 days. By the fourth day, the sprouts are ready.

Sprouts Can Be Used As

a) Fillings in sandwiches, omelettes, cutlets, *dosas*
b) Can be eaten raw — mixed with chopped onions and lemon juice
c) Used in curd
d) Used in soups
e) Steamed

Soyabean and Its Products

Nutritive Value

a)	Appreciable amount of good quality protein	7	gm / 100 gm
b)	Higher calories	420	cal / 100 gm
c)	Contains unsaturated fat (helps in lowering cholesterol)	20	mg / 100 gm
d)	High fibre content	4	gm / 100 gm
e)	Appreciable amount of iron	10	mg / 100 gm
f)	Mineral content	4.5	gm / 100 gm
g)	Vitamins A and B complex		

Soyabean Can Be Used For

a) Sprouts
b) Curry
c) Dhokla*
d) *Dosa*

Mushrooms

Nutritive Value

a)	High in good quality protein	10 gm/100 gm
b)	Low calories	40 cal/100 gm
c)	Low fat	1 gm/100 gm
d)	Low in carbohydrate	4 gm/100 gm

* Dhokla – A spongy delight made of gram flour

e) Amount of Fibre 0.4 gm/100 gm
f) Iron content 1.6 mg/100 gm

It Can Be Used For

a) Soups
b) Fillings
c) Salads
d) Vegetables

Leafy Vegetables

(Spinach, fenugreek, amaranth, coriander, cabbage)

Nutritive Value 70 cal/100 gm

a) High dietary fibre
b) Appreciable amounts of Vitamins A and C
c) Iron and other micro-minerals are also present

It Can Be Used For

a) Salads
b) Soups
c) Fillings
d) Mixed with curd (*raita*)

Wheat–Gram Flour

Wheat 80 gm + black gram 20 gm

Comparison of nutritive value of wheat flour and wheat–gram flour.

		Wheat–gram Flour	*Wheat Flour*
a)	Protein	All 15.5 gm/100 gm	Some 11.8 gm/100 gm
b)	Fat	3.5 gm	1.5 gm
c)	Carbohydrate	65.0 gm	70.0 gm
d)	Fibre	1.2 gm	0.9 gm

It Can Be Used For

a) Unleavened bread
b) Bread

UNIT III

EXERCISE — LIVE LONGER FEEL YOUNGER

Exercise and Its Benefits

Exercise helps in reducing blood sugar, in burning calories and thus reducing weight; in reducing blood pressure, toning of heart muscles, improving blood circulation and increasing good HDL cholesterol and lowering bad LDL cholesterol. More importantly, it brings an increased sense of well-being and better quality of life. Thus exercise becomes an essential part of treatment planning especially for patients with diabetes, obesity and heart disease. Exercise is also essential for healthy persons as regular exercise helps to keep away from these diseases. There are some additional benefits of exercise such as one remains vigorous even at old age, it prevents spondylosis and joint problems and finally it improves the quality of life and gives mental relaxation.

Some Principles of Exercise

If you find any difficulty in pursuing any physical activity, it is better to get your heart and respiratory organs checked up.

One has to be careful while starting an exercise. It helps you in the following ways:

1. Gives you a sense of well-being
2. Ensures a more disciplined life
3. Offers mental relaxation
4. Helps in keeping your weight within normal range
5. Improves your digestion
6. Lowers blood sugar

7. Lowers circulating fats like cholesterol and triglycerides
8. Reduces the dose of drugs you are taking; some drugs can even be eliminated
9. Improves your heart and respiratory reserve

If there are so many advantages, why not start an exercise or game right now taking all necessary precautions.

Once you have continued for a month or so, try to evaluate how much benefit you have got.

If you are convinced about its usefulness try to rope in others too. You will be doing some social service.

Points to Remember Regarding Exercise

1. Increase the intensity and duration of exercise gradually.
2. Do not let exercise lead to severe physical exhaustion.
3. Correct footwear (sports shoes) is absolutely essential while exercising.
4. Do not exercise immediately after meals.
5. Do not exercise if fasting and blood glucose is above 300 mg/dl or in presence of urea in urine (ketonuria).
6. Exercise regularly at least 5 days a week.

The best forms of exercise for persons above the age of 30 years are brisk walking, slow jogging, bicycling, gardening, floor exercises, outdoor games like tennis, indoor games like badminton and swimming.

Intensity of the exercise is measured in terms of the percentage of patient's maximum heart rate (MHR). It is calculated by a simple formula (MHR = 220 – age of the patient). Intensity of the exercise should be gradually increased to reach heart rate (Pulse rate) about 70% of MHR, eg, for a 50 yrs old man the target heart rate should be 120/minute (MHR 220 – 50 = 170, 70% of this = 120).

It is commonly seen that after playing two games of badminton or swimming for half an hour, on the way to home, one stops at the roadside restaurant to reward oneself. Although exercise burns calories, one plate of dosa quickly makes up the deficit. Brisk walking for 45 minutes at least five days a week is in my opinion the best form of exercise. It should cover the distance of 4 to 5 km in this time. Yoga exercise (Yogasanas) are good for relaxation and meditation and should be done in addition to brisk walking if time permits. There is no time for exercise in my busy schedule – is a common excuse, given by patients. They should be motivated to squeeze some time out for exercise.

Calories Burnt in Various Activities

Activity	*Calories burnt in 30 mins*	*Activity*	*Calories burnt in 30 mins*
Self		**Recreational**	
Resting in bed	30	Painting	60
Sitting	36	Driving Car	84
Standing relaxed	42	Dancing	165
House Work		***Other Physical Activities***	
Sweeping floor	51	Walking average	108
Washing clothes	90	Cycling	175
Ironing clothes	126	Swimming	350
Mopping the floor	126	Running 10 km/hr	400

Remember you require to burn 7,500 calories to lose 1 kg body weight.

Studies show that doing several daily workouts of 10 to 15 minutes can be as effective for losing weight as exercising all in one chunk of time: You tend to exercise longer — by the week's end than in a single session.

Walking

Walking is a simple exercise yet as powerful and proven a therapy as customized diets and medication. So, why do people not do it more often? Why do so many take it up enthusiastically and then give it up half way?

May be they have not been using the right strategy. Did you know that there are different types of walking personalities? Customizing your walks to fit you will help you enjoy and also help you stick to your workouts. Best of all, you will reduce pounds — faster and easier.

You do not mind exercising but hate to do it alone. Your ideal partner could be your best friend or neighbour.

Here is how to make your walks more social and boost your workouts when you are in a group.

- **Find a partner.** Just ask. That is usually all it takes to find someone to walk with you. Two partners are better that one: more lively conversation, and, if one cannot make it, you have a backup. If you are running short of walking buddies, put up a notice in your building. You will never run short of volunteers this way.
- **Make it a routine.** Choose the best days and times that will work for both you and your partner; pen it in your weekly planner.
- **Make it challenging.** Choose a long, steep trail so that you can catch up on the past week's happenings as you expend extra calories.
- **Follow the leader.** Alternate the responsibility for planning your course. You may lead a steed session one week, while your partner chooses a hilly slope the next.
- **Walk with dogs.** If you do not have your own, volunteer to walk a friend's dog. You may make new (four-legged) friends. The more positive reinforcement and fun you have, the more you will walk — and the more weight you will lose.

The Romantic

You love exploring wooded trails or interesting streets. Although your walks are often times for self-reflection, you also enjoy strolls with your spouse at sunset.

Do not wait for weekends to discover inspiring places to walk. Here are some ways to make your everyday route more fulfilling.

- **Locate interesting places.** Venture down side streets that you usually zip by on your way to somewhere else. Notice intricate landscapes, buildings with history, beautiful gardens, unique decorations — and steal a few ideas for your home.

- **Collect beautiful picture.** Carry a camera to capture a splendid landscape, a cluster of wildflowers or a marble water fountain. Your photos will also serve as reminders of the pleasure of walking.
- **Keep a journal.** Jot down your thoughts and feelings after a walk. Reviewing it later will make you want to repeat it. When you are interested in your surroundings or in tune with your thoughts, you are likely to walk longer and sustain a brisker pace.

Personal Views

Walking – the simplest and the most effective form of exercise.

Let us find out how some real people have lost weight and gotten healthier with this 'mundane' activity.

Mr A (Age 30, Businessman)

"I was overweight. I had high cholesterol levels combined with uncontrollable blood pressure. For a man of my age these were dangerous signals. I was forced to take charge of my health. I joined a gym, and initially the walks served as a warm up or cool down. Now I see them as much more — I feel mentally fit and alert when I take a walk. So they've become an addiction, and when I don't go out, I feel uneasy and incomplete."

Mr B (Age 40, Restaurant Owner)

"Lack of commitment, high costs and overcrowdedness were my reasons for not joining a gym. But exercise was a must because I was entering middle age, which is the time when most health problems creep in and I was already overweight. Walking not only knocked off my extra pounds but also became a source of recreation. In fact, I love it so much that now even the rains do not deter me!"

Mr F (Age 75, Businessman)

"My goal — to stay healthy. My style — to walk. I have been going for one-hour-ten-minute walks daily for the past 20 years. My usual routine on leaving office is to first go to the park and then go home. I have even motivated my friends and wife to walk. When I started, there were few gyms in Mumbai, so the best workout was a simple walk. I walk alone because I enjoy humming hymns while walking."

UNIT IV

FOOD EXCHANGES

Eating for maintaining good health does not mean to be on a monotonous and rigid diet. Eating is one of the great pleasures in life and it is possible to eat well and enjoy eating. Correct choice and quantity of foods would go a long way in maintaining optimal health.

The 'exchange system' is applicable to all types of food groups. Seven exchanges are used: milk, vegetables, cereals, pulses, fruits, meat and fats/oils. The meal planning is simplified by grouping foods into exchange lists. Each item within an exchange has the same amount of protein, fat, carbohydrate and calories in the portion specified as any other item in that list, for instance, one 'cereal exchange' equals 18 gms of carbohydrates, 2.5 gms of protein and 85 calories. One large slice of bread is equal to one cereal exchange, as also two Marie biscuits or 3 tablespoons of rice flakes. Hence foods in any one group can be substituted for foods within the same group though the portion/size may not be the same. But foods in one group usually cannot be traded for foods in another group.

Hence, foods included in the meals should be calculated, using exchange lists. This requires careful planning and some practice. If followed diligently the exchange lists aid in introducing variety in diet.

The weighing scale is necessary. However, it is easier to express quantities in terms of household measures than to use an accurate weighing scale.

Commonly Used Home Measurements

One level teaspoon:	5 gms
One level tablespoon:	15 gms
One cup:	150 ml

Table 4.1: Approximate Measures of Some Foodstuffs

	Items	*Measurement*	*Weight*
1.	A medium-sized chapati	8" in diameter 0.1" thickness	20 gms
2.	A medium slice of sponge cake or of spongy delight	2¼" x 1¾" x ¾"	25 gms
3.	Bread: medium	3" x 2¾" x 0.4"	25 gms
	large	4¼" x 3½" x 0.5"	35 gms

Measurement of a Cup

1 cup = 150 ml
Diameter of top 2¼"
Diameter of bottom 2"
Depth 4"

It is always advisable to weigh and measure proportions till one is able to judge the serving size visually.

While planning the meals with the help of food exchange, one can take care of the patient's overall health, especially by increasing the amount of fibre and decreasing cholesterol and saturated fats in the diet.

Exchange List of Different Food Groups

Cereal Exchange

This lists the amount of raw cereals and their preparations for substituting foods of equal value in exchange.

One exchange of cereal contains:

Carbohydrate	18 gms
Protein	02.5 gms
Calories	85 cal

Food		*Amount*
Barley	25 gms	2 level tablespoons
Sorghum (*jowar*)	25 gms	" " "
Maize (dry) corn	25 gms	" " "
Popcorn (without fat)	30 gms	2 cups
Oatmeal	25 gms	2 level tablespoons
Ragi		25 gms
Rice	35 gms	" " "
Flaked rice (poha)	25 gms	½ cup
Puffed rice (murmura)	25 gms	¾ cup
Semolina (rava)	25 gms	2½ level tablespoons
Wheat flour (atta)	25 gms	" " "
Wheat flour (*atta*)	25 gms	2 heaped tablespoons
Refined flour (*maida*)	25 gms	" " "
Bread	35 gms	1 large slice
Arrowroot biscuits	3	
Marie biscuits	14 gms	4 in number
Cream crackers	-	3 in number
Salted biscuits	17 gms	5 in number
Sponge cake	28 gms	
Macaroni	25 gms	½ cup or 2½ level tablespoons
Spaghetti	25 gms	" " "
Cornflakes	20 gms	½ cup
Cornflour	20 gms	2½ cup level tablespoon

Note:

1) Ragi and bajra are rich sources of calcium and iron respectively.
2) Researchers believe that ragi is beneficial for diabetics, however scientific proof is awaited.
3) Wholemeal flour is more nutritious than refined flour, because its fibre content is appreciably high.

Legumes and Pulse Exchange

This gives out the types and amount of raw legumes and pulses for substituting food of equal value in exchange.

One exchange of legumes and pulses contains:

Carbohydrates	15 gms
Protein	6 gms
Calories	85 cal

Food		*Amount*		
Bengal gram pulse (*chana dal*)	25 gms	2 level tablespoons		
Roasted chana	25 gms	"	"	"
Cowpeas (*barbati lobia*)	25 gms	"	"	"
Black gram pulse (*urad dal*)	25 gms	"	"	"
Green gram (*mung dal*)	25 gms	"	"	"
Horse gram (*kulthi*)	25 gms	"	"	"
Lentil (*masoor*)	25 gms	"	"	"
Moth beans	25 gms	"	"	"
Dried Peas (dry *matar*)	25 gms	"	"	"
Kidney beans (*rajmah*)	25 gms	"	"	"
Yellow lentil pulse (*arhar dal*)	25 gms	"	"	"
Soyabean	20 gms	"	"	"
Bean sprouts	77 gms	2½ cups		

Note:

1) 20 gms soyabean contains 12 gms of protein and 6 gms of carbohydrate. Soyabean is a versatile food item for vegetarian diabetics.
2) Sprouts are easier to digest. It has high vitamin content, low calorie value and provides bulk to the diet.

Vegetable Exchange

Vegetables are grouped into three types:

1. Group A: Leafy Vegetables
2. Group B: Roots and Tubers
3. Group C: Other Vegetables

1. *Group A: Leafy Vegetables*

This list gives the amount of raw vegetables for substituting foods of equal value in exchange.

One exchange of vegetable in group A contains:

Carbohydrate	4	gms
Protein	1	gm
Calories	40	

Foods	*Amount*
Amaranth (*choulai*)	93 gms
Bengal gram leaves (*chana sag*)	38 gms
Bottlegourd leaves (*louki ka sag*)	102 gms
Cauliflower greens (*phool gobhi ka sag*)	61 gms
Colocasia leaves (*arbi*)	71 gms
Coriander leaves (*hara dhania*)	64 gms
Cowpea leaves	105 gms
Drumstick leaves (*saijan ke patte*)	33 gms
Fenugreek leaves (*methi*)	48 gms
Ipomea leaves (*kahni sag*)	143 gms
Khol-khol greens (*ganth gobhi*)	68 gms
Lettuce (salad *patte*)	126 gms
Mint leaves (*pudina patte*)	38 gms
Mustard leaves	118 gms
Neem leaves (mature)	31 gms
Neem leaves (tender)	25 gms
Pumpkin leaves (*kumhra sag*)	70 gms
Radish leaves (*mooli ke patte*)	143 gms
Rapeseed leaves (*sarson ka sag*)	83 gms
Spinach (*palak*)	134 gms
Soya leaves (*soya sag*)	56 gms
Tamarind leaves, tender (*imli patta*)	35 gms
Turnip green (*shalgam ka sag*)	30 gms

Note:

1. These vegetables may be used liberally as their carbohydrate and calorie content is low.
2. Neem, fenugreek have been advocated in the treatment of diabetes. Their exact mode of action is still unknown.
3. Most of the vegetables of this group are rich sources of calcium, iron and vitamins, therefore their consumption should be encouraged.

2. *Group B: Roots and Tubers*

This list shows the amount of raw vegetables for substituting food items of equal value in exchange.

One exchange of vegetables in group B contains:

Carbohydrate	10 gms
Protein	2 gms
Calories	25

Food	*Amount*
Beetroot (*chukander*)	94 gms
Colocasia (*arbi*)	46 gms
Onion	90 gms
Parsnip	45 gms
Sweet potato (*shakarkandi*)	35 gms
Tapioca	30 gms
Yam (*zimikand*)	57 gms
Double beans (*chastang*)	54 gms
Carrot (*gajar*)	79 gms
Lotus root (*kamal kakari*)	75 gms

Note:

1. 50 gms of tapioca contains 20 gms carbohydrate and 54 calories.
2. It is recommended that the consumption of group B vegetables be restricted as they are rich in carbohydrates.

3. *Group C: Other Vegetables*

This list shows the types of vegetables for substituting food of equal value in exchange.

One exchange of group C vegetables contains:

Carbohydrate	9	gms
Protein	2	gms
Calories	40	

Food	*Amount*
Turnip (*shalgam*)	90 gms
Ash gourd (*petha*)	268 gms
Bittergourd (*karela*)	155 gms
Bottlegourd (*lauki*)	287 gms
Brinjal (*baingan*)	152 gms
Broad beans	73 gms
Cauliflower (*phool gobhi*)	93 gms
Drumstick (*saijan ki phali*)	128 gms
Field beans (tender)	76 gms
French beans	145 gms
Capsicum (*shimla mirch*)	162 gms
Jackfruit, tender (*kathal*)	78 gms
Khol khol (*ganth gobhi*)	141 gms
Lady's finger (*bhindi*)	96 gms
Mango, green (*aam*)	65 gms
Papaya green (*papita*)	190 gms
Parwal	190 gms
Peas (*matar*)	23 gms
Pumpkin (*kaddu*)	126 gms
Rape plant stem (*sarson ki dandi*)	138 gms
Tinda	189 gms
Tomato, green	170 gms
*Mushrooms	100 gms

* Mushroom: protein content is 4.3 gms and carbohydrate is 4 gms per 100 gms.

Note:

1. *Karela* is recommended for diabetics, however it is being researched on.
2. Liberal servings of vegetables of group C can be used. They add bulk to the diet and increase the satiable value of food.

Fruit Exchange

The list gives the amount of raw fruits for substituting food of equal value in exchange.

One exchange of fruit contains

Carbohydrate	10 gms
Calories	50

Fruits	*Amount*
Gooseberry (*amla*)	77 gms
Apple (*seb*)	76 gms
Apricots, fresh	81 gms
Bael fruit (*bel*)	23 gms
Banana, ripe (*kela*)	32 gms
Cherries, red	69 gms
Dates, dried (*khajur*)	14 gms
Dates, fresh	35 gms
Figs (*anjeer*)	134 gms
Grapes (*angoor*)	70 gms
Guava (*amrud*)	99 gms
Jackfruit, ripe (*kathal*)	60 gms
Jambu fruit (*jamun*)	60 gms
Lemon (*bara nimbu*)	88 gms
Litchi	56 gms
Lemon, sweet (*malta*)	104 gms
Lime, sweet (*mausambi*)	83 gms
Loquat (*lokat*)	89 gms
Mango, ripe (*aam*)	50 gms

Watermelon (*tarbuj*)	243 gms
Neem fruit	67 gms
Orange (*santara*)	70 gms
Papaya, ripe (*papita*)	117 gms
Peaches (*aadoo*)	38 gms
Pears (*nashpati*)	81 gms
Pineapple (*ananas*)	65 gms
Plum (*alubokhara*)	85 gms
Pomegranate (*anar*)	52 gms
Raisins (*kishmish*)	17 gms
Raspberry (*rusbhary*)	90 gms
Sapota (*chiku*)	43 gms
Strawberry	109 gms
Tomato, ripe (*tamatar*)	250 gms
Woodapple (*kaith*)	20 gms

Milk Exchange

This list gives the types and amount of milk and its preparations for substituting food item of equal value in exchange.

One exchange of milk contains:

Carbohydrate	5 gms
Protein	5 gms
Fat	6 gms
Calories	100

Food	*Amount*
DMS*/MD** milk	166 ml
Milk (buffalo)	85 ml
Milk (cow)	150 ml
Curd (cow's milk)	170 ml
Buttermilk	670 ml
Skimmed milk	345 ml
Cottage cheese	30 gms
Khoa (buffalo's milk)	25 gms

Skimmed milk powder	25 gms
Whole milk powder	20 gms
Soya milk	276 ml
Soya milk cheese (tofu)	20 gms

Note:

1. The protein and carbohydrate content of these items is high.
2. The measurement of a cup holding 150 ml of liquid has

Diameter at the top	2¼"
Diameter at the bottom	2"
Depth	4"

3. Soymilk and its products are highly nutritive.

* DMS—Delhi Milk Scheme

**MD—Mother Dairy

Meat Exchange

Meat exchange is grouped into two:

Group I: Low fat meat (less than 4% fat)

Group II: Medium fat meat (4–8% fat)

Group I

This list gives the amount of raw low fat meat and other protein rich foods for substituting equal value in exchange.

One exchange of lean meat contains:

Protein	15 gms
Calories	80

Type	*Amount*
Beef: tender beef, ribs, steak	70 gms
Lamb: exclude breast	32 gms
Veal: exclude breast	35 gms
Poultry: exclude goose	53 gms
Lean mutton	45 gms
Fish: sardine, mackerel, herring, pomfret white	70 gms

Other seafood:	lobster	89 gms
	prawn	40 gms
	crab	93 gms
Cheese: with less than 2% butter fat		24 gms

Group II

This list gives the amount of raw medium fat meat and other protein-rich foods for substituting equal value in exchange.

One exchange of medium fat meat contains:

Protein	15 gms
Calories	85

Type	*Amount*
Pork: loin, shoulder, butt	20 gms
Mutton	40 gms
Liver, goat	75 gms
Pigeon	50 gms
Sausage	25 gms
Ham (shredded)	30 gms
Seafood:	
small crabs	47 gms
shrimps, small dried	23 gms
Egg (hen)	50 gms (1 in number)
Egg yolk (concentrated source of cholesterol)	55 gms
Cheese made from whole milk	24 gms

Note: *Breast of lamb, veal and beef are high fat meats. Their fat content varies between 8 and 15 %*

Fat/Oil Exchange

This list gives the amount of fat/oil containing foods for substituting equal value in exchange.

One exchange of fat contains:

Fat	8 gms
Calories	90

Type	*Amount*
* Vegetable oil, safflower oil, sunflower oil, corn oil, soya oil, cotton seed oil, rice bran oil.	10 gms, 2 teaspoons
Olive oil, sesame oil, groundnut oil/coconut oil, mustard oil	10 gms, 2 teaspoons
Clarified Butter	10 gms, 2 teaspoons
Margarine	12.5 gms, 2½ teaspoons
Lard	12.5 gms, 2½ teaspoons
Cream	20 gms, 2 teaspoons
Butter	12 gms
Nuts	15 – 20 gms 10 – 12 in number
Mayonnaise	12 gms

* *These are unsaturated fats. Their consumption is recommended instead of saturated fat but in moderations.*

UNIT V

WEIGHT CONTROL

Losing Weight Sensibly

Obesity is a health hazard for persons of all ages. An overweight person has a shorter life expectancy and is more prone to diseases of the heart, liver and kidney. If you are overweight you are also more accident-prone and are likely to get diabetes and other degenerative problems along with the emotional pressure of not looking your best. A heavy person also finds it difficult to face our slim-trim-lean oriented society. The good news, however, is that all these hazards disappear along with the excess weight.

Overweight refers to the state of having 20 per cent more weight than that indicated by the optimum desirable weight tables. Exceptions to this rule are muscular athletes and people who are overweight because of their muscle weight.

It is, in fact, surprising that one individual's metabolism can burn up any amount of calories without putting on an ounce of excess fat on the body, whereas another person eats very little and finds it all turning to fat. Such metabolic differences between individuals have a lot to do with overweight.

If a child is overfed or introduced to solid carbohydrate foods early in life, a large number of fat cells build up in the body. Later, he will have a greater tendency to get fat and to stay that way. Bottle-fed babies tend to be fatter than the breast-fed babies when they grow up. Genetic factors, though poorly understood, may play a role. A child of overweight parents is more likely to become fat than the offspring of lean parents.

The conveniences produced by the technological explosion have significantly decreased calorie output. Modern transportation results in less walking. Few people will walk up and down the stairs when there is a lift. Lack of nutritional knowledge leads to an unwise selection of food and is a major factor in causing obesity. Whatever the etiology of obesity, the cause of obesity is always an imbalance of calorie intake from food and calorie expenditure by the body.

There are no secret formulas for slimming. Diet pills used for curbing appetite are not advisable as they greatly disturb the emotional balance too.

Calorie is the amount of energy in any food which our body uses up for various activities. When we take in too many calories, the excess is stored as fat instead of being burnt away.

Treatment of Obesity

Prevention is the best form of treatment. Balancing the calorie content of the diet to the needs of the person at all stages in life is the only way to prevent abnormal weight gain.

Determination

Be determined to lose weight. Once you are determined, successful dieting will help to control appetite—a diet that supplies the body with less energy than it burns up. A good workable exercise programme and relaxation technique to deal with stress helps your determination.

Diet

Diet remains the cornerstone of therapy for all forms of obesity. Dietary treatment involves lowering the calorie intake below that of calorie expenditure. Unless a person is excessively overweight, it is sufficient to lose fat at the rate of 1/2(half) kg per week. Small weekly weight losses can be achieved by following a prudent diet in which portions of each food item are decreased and highly concentrated calorie foods are omitted. Reduction of alcohol intake is an important element of a sensible diet.

Keeping Count of Calories

The most common form of weight control is counting calories. It is very simple: when energy output exceeds energy input, fat is reduced.

How to Work Out Calories

Each ounce ie, 28.35 gm of stored fat provides about 250 calories of energy. So if you need 2,800 calories a day but are eating only 2,300 calories you will have a calorie deficit of 500 calories. This means you should lose about ½ to ¾ kg a week. If you want to lose more, you simply decrease the calorie intake.

It is important to lose weight gradually, rather than starving yourself. Nutritional consideration is very important in meal planning, else you could end up with a slim waistline but bad skin, rough hair, weakness or some illness.

Thumb Rule for Calculating Ideal Body Weight (IBW)

The ideal body weight (IBW) in kgs can be calculated by subtracting 100 from his/her height (in cms). For example IBW of a person with 160 cm height is 60 kgs (160 – 100). Twenty per cent above IBW is overweight while, 20 per cent below IBW is underweight. Based on these lines, the daily calorie requirements can be worked out.

Guidelines for Reducing Weight

If you are among the overweight and decide it is time to do something about it, I suggest you first take an opinion from your physician. However, if you have only a few kilos to shed, you can safely do it alone, by following the guidelines offered below. Beware of being taken in by promises of shortcut ways to slimness and remember that dieting has become big business. There are diet clinics and diet books advocating every imaginable way to lose weight — 'quick weight loss programme'. Many of these 'fad' diets are nothing else than 'planned' malnutrition. It would not be surprising that once the diet is terminated, the lost weight is promptly replaced. Be realistic. There are no miracle methods of shedding extra calories, especially if you intend to keep them off forever.

a) In any calorie-controlled diet you need to be sure to have plenty of green leafy vegetables in the form of salads.

b) Make one meal a day of a 'vegetable salad' made of a variety of raw vegetables such as carrots, tomatoes, lettuce, cabbage, cucumber, celery and other greens tossed together. Use a low calorie salad dressing like vinegar, lemon juice or curd. This will fulfil your vitamin and mineral needs as well.

c) Have one or two pieces of fruit a day.

d) A good helping of lean protein food such as meat, fish, poultry or low fat cheese should be taken.

e) Wholegrain cereals should be taken for roughage and valuable B complex vitamins.

f) If you suffer from constipation, add three or four teaspoons of bran to your food.

g) Do not add fats to foods unnecessarily. Bake or poach instead of frying.

h) The diet must be easily adaptable to use easily available foods.

i) The diet should be such as to be used for a long time to attain the desired weight loss.

j) Maximum weight loss should not be more than 1 kg per week.

k) Exercise helps to expend calories and increase body efficiency.

l) The diet should be one that the entire family can help the person with.

m) Avoid all high calorie starchy foods like biscuits, cakes, pastries, sweets and alcohol. These are empty foods without any real nutritional value. Look for low calorie alternatives to everything.

n) The key to success is perseverance. Set a daily or weekly calorie allowance and stick to it. Record everything you eat and drink, in a notebook. It helps to keep track. Weigh yourself every week and record the results after waking up but before you get dressed.

Behaviour Modification

Behaviour therapy or modification is a new concept in weight control that focuses on changing habits and lifestyle on a long-term basis. The focus is not solely on eating but also on knowledge, misconceptions, activity time management and life stresses. The programme stresses on the controls of the hows, whys and whens of eating. Here are a few guidelines of behaviour modification.

Keep a Food Intake Sheet

Keep track of what you eat for a week or two. Your record should be very detailed.

Try to Pinpoint Your Eating Problems

Check your eating speed. Also record places where you eat, how much and when.

Make Eating an Enjoyable Experience

Learn to eat so that you can savour the joy of eating. Avoid television, newspapers or any other distractions while you eat. Eat slowly by taking small bites, tasting each morsel carefully. For snacking problems create an alternative set of activities at the time you usually snack like walking, painting or any other hobby.

Reduce Temptations

Make a shopping list and purchase only those things that are on the list.

Seek Your Family's Support

Explain your plans to them and seek their support. Request that snacks be reduced between meals.

Cope with Emotions

Do not eat when you are upset, anxious or angry. Try jogging or going for a walk when these emotions creep in.

Gradually Lose Weight

Aim at a gradual weight loss. Keep a record and remember, there is no need to starve yourself.

Do Your Exercise

Make a regular exercise pattern, whether it is jogging, calisthenics, aerobics, walking or playing a game.

Special Functions

If you are going to a party, wedding or a social get-together, eat something substantial before you leave the house so that you do not arrive at the function hungry. To avoid temptation, keep yourself busy in socialising instead of keeping a watchful eye on the eats!

These rules apply to everyone but habit changes should be individually worked out. For instance, some persons can easily eliminate foods while others cannot.

A constant eater should satisfy his or her needs with a handy and substantial supply of high-bulk low-calorie foods such as celery, carrots, cucumber, raw cabbage, cauliflower, radishes, apples, greens. This would help avoid consumption of high calorie foods at meal times.

Change Shopping Habits — A Necessity

a) Shop only from a prepared list and stick to it.
b) Shop after eating or at least when you are not hungry.
c) Resist the free snacks offered at the supermarket and confectioners.
d) Buy fresh fruits rather than fruits canned with sugar.
e) Choose canned or frozen vegetables that are plain instead of those containing rich sauces. Fresh vegetables, of course, are the best.

Change Cooking Habits

a) Trim all fat from meat before cooking.
b) Boil meat that you would normally fry. Marinate chicken or meat using a low-calorie dressing like vinegar, lemon, garlic or curd.
c) When baking fish or meat, use lemon juice instead of butter or fat.
d) Use lean meat in all non-vegetarian recipes. Before cooking chicken, remove the skin and any loose fat.
e) Cook vegetables in a small amount of water with herbs and spices instead of butter.

f) Use whipped butter for use in sandwiches or for spreads because the air it contains reduces the fat content and also reduces the calories considerably.
g) Learn which are the low or no calorie foods and serve them often in meals and snacks, such as raw vegetables for salads.

Exercise

Exercise is an essential part of appetite and weight control. A good weight reduction programme includes regulation of energy output as well as calorie intake. It also increases the metabolic efficiency. (*Refer to Unit III*)

Table 5.1: Foods Allowed and Foods Forbidden when Dieting

Foods Allowed	*Amount*	*Foods not Allowed*
I. Bread and Cereal Group		Cakes, pastries,
Bread (brown)	1 slice daily	noodles, macaroni
II. Pulses and Legumes		
Bengal gram, black gram, green gram, yellow lentil, lentils, soyabeans (whole as well as husked dal are preparable)	2 cups cooked daily	
III. Milk and Meat Products		
Milk, curd (skimmed)	2 cups	Whole milk, cream,
Buttermilk, whey	1 glass	butter, cheese
Cottage cheese	20 gms	(other than cottage)
Chicken	a serving (20 gms)	
Lean meat	a serving	Pork, fish with lots of fat (tuna and
Lean fish prepared without fat	a serving	salmon)
Egg (boiled or poached)	1 per day	

Foods Allowed	*Amount*	*Foods not Allowed*
IV. Fruit and Vegetables		
Amaranth, spinach, drumstick leaves, fenugreek leaves, coriander leaves, brinjal, lady's finger, capsicum, beans, onions, drumstick, cabbage, cucumber, cauliflower, carrots	Substantial proportions	
Tomatoes, colocasia, potatoes	In moderation	
Fresh citrus fruits — guava, papaya, water-melon	1 serving daily	Sapota, banana, mango
V. Miscellaneous		
Spices and condiments	In moderation	No gravy
Lemon	Substantial proportions	sauces, oil dressing
Artificial sweetener	As per taste	
Tea, coffee, clear broth or soups, fresh lime, soda, coconut water, jaljeera, kanji	Substantial proportions	Pickles, nuts, aerated drinks, alcoholic beverages

Shedding Excess Weight through Substitution

You will be surprised to know how much a small quantity of some foods such as butter, oil and sugar add to our calories, and how it takes a much larger amount of others such as vegetables, skimmed milk and its products to equal the same number of calories. A calorie substitution chart for different kinds of foods is an important guide for dieters. You may not always realise how quickly calories add up at meal times. Here is a sample of how calorie intake can be reduced through sensible substitution.

Table 5.2 : Menus with Sensible Substitution

BREAKFAST

From This	*Calories*	*Substitute with*	*Calories*
½ glass whole milk	70	½ glass skimmed milk or ½ glass butter milk	25 15
1 scrambled egg	120	1 boiled egg	78
1 piece of processed cheese (20 gm)	150	Same amount of cottage cheese (uncreamed)	60
2 teaspoons butter	100	2 teaspoons white butter or whipped cream	50
A cup of coffee with a teaspoon of sugar and 2 teaspoons of cream	110	A cup of coffee with low calorie sweetener and made of skimmed milk	30
2 slices of white bread	120	2 slices of brown bread made of whole cereals	70
Total Calories	670	Total Calories	298

MID-MORNING SNACKS

From This	*Calories*	*Substitute with*	*Calories*
A cup of coffee with a spoon of sugar and 2 teaspoons cream	110	A cup of coffee with low calorie sweetener and made of skimmed milk	30
1 small pastry	140	2 low calorie bran biscuits or cream crackers	20
A big apple	80	A small apple or A green apple	50 20
Total Calories	330	Total Calories	120

LUNCH

From This	*Calories*	*Substitute with*	*Calories*
Red meat with potatoes cooked in tomato gravy	350	Lean meat stewed and baked with lemon juice	150
Mixed vegetables made of colocasia and carrots	160	Spinach/ amaranth/ fenugreek	30
A cup of whole milk curd	170	Skimmed milk curd with grated cucumber	40
Salad with oil dressing	170	Raw salad	20
2 chapatis with ghee	180	2 chapatis made of gramflour bran or wheatflour, without ghee	100
Total Calories	1030	Total Calories	340

EVENING SNACKS

From This	*Calories*	*Substitute with*	*Calories*
An aerated drink	200	1 glass fresh lime water, without sugar	Nil
1 cup of custard prepared from whole milk with 2 teaspoons sugar	205	Green gram sprouts with lemon, coriander, chillies, salt and spices	50
Total Calories	405	Total Calories	50

DINNER

From This	*Calories*	*Substitute with*	*Calories*
Tomato soup with fried breadcrumbs	200	Thin vegetable soup without breadcrumbs	30
20 gm chicken made with skin	500	20 gm chicken prepared with skin removed	250
½ cup of washed potatoes	125	Brinjal made with tamarind	60
A cup of fried rice	220	A cup of boiled rice with starch removed	110

2 slices of white bread	120	2 chapatis without ghee	100
½ cup semolina kheer made of whole milk and a teaspoon of sugar	205	½ cup of semolina kheer made of skimmed milk and artificial sweetener	110
Total Calories	1370	Total Calories	670

BEVERAGES

From This	*Calories*	*Substitute with*	*Calorie*
1 glass whole milk	170	Skimmed milk or buttermilk	80
Aerated drink	200	Fresh lime or coconut water	Nil
		1 glass aerated water ie soda	Nil
Coffee (with cream) with 2 teaspoons sugar	110	Coffee with skimmed milk and artificial sweetener	30
Cocoa with 2 teaspoons sugar and 1 glass of whole milk	220	Cocoa with artificial sweetener and ½ glass skimmed milk and ½ glass water	60
Beer 240 ml	98	Liquor 20 ml with water/soda	50
Total Calories	798	Total Calories	220

BREAKFAST FOODS

From This	*Calories*	*Substitute with*	*Calories*
Rice flakes 1 cup	110	Puffed rice 1 cup	50
2 eggs (scrambled)	220	2 eggs boiled (poached)	160
Butter on toast	170	White butter on brown bread	120
Processed cheese	105	Cheese cottage uncreamed 20 gm	30
Total Calories	606	Total Calories	360

DESSERTS

From This	*Calories*	*Substitute with*	*Calories*
2 pieces plain cake	110	2 pieces sponge cake	40
2 pieces chocolate cake with icing	425	2 pieces sponge cake with icing	120
2 pieces fruit cake	115	1 cup grapes	65
2 pieces almond cake	220	2 plums	50
Cookies 1 piece	120	1 Marie biscuit	20
Ice-cream 1 cup	170	Flavoured yoghurt or curd sweetened with artificial sweetener	60
Pudding (flavoured) ½ cup	140	½ cupPudding (dietetic non-fat milk)	60
Custard 1 cup	220	1 small guava	40
Total Calories	1520	Total Calories	455

MISCELLANEOUS

From This	*Calories*	*Substitute with*	*Calories*
Chicken			
20 gm chicken with skin	350	20 gm chicken without skin	175
Meat			
20 gm red meat	250	20 gm lean meat	150
Potatoes			
1 cup fried	480	Baked	100
1 cup mashed	245	Boiled	110
Salads			
Salad with 1 tablespoon of oil dressing,	180	Raw salad with vinegar/lemon	20
Salad with 1 tablespoon of mayonnaise,	125		
Salad with 1 tablespoon of French dressing,	105	Salad with low calorie or dietetic dressing	40
Sandwiches			
Club sandwiches	375	Tomato and cucumber	150
With butter and jam	275	Boiled egg white	150
Snacks			
Peanuts salted, 40 gms	170	Rice crackers, 40 gm	5
Peanuts roasted in oil, 40 gms	375	Grapes 1 cup or 1 apple	65
Potato chips 10 (medium)	115	Cracker or low fat sweet	10

Soups			
Chicken soup with 1 tablespoon cream,	210	Chicken noodle soup, 1 cup	110
1 cup Tomato soup with fried breadcrumbs and 1 spoon butter	210	Plain thin vegetarian soup (broth)	20
Vegetables			
Baked beans, 1 cup	320	Green beans (boiled), 1 cup	30
Corn canned, 1 cup	185	Cauliflower (boiled), 1 cup	30
Peas, 1 cup (canned)	145	Peas (fresh) (boiled), 1 cup	115
		Spinach (boiled), 1 cup	40
Total Calories	4115	Total Calories	1320

Table 5.3 : Weight Reduction Diet (1000 Calories a Day)

Either	Or
Breakfast	
1 glass of skimmed milk	1 glass of buttermilk,
Boiled egg with tomato	Cottage cheese, sandwiches
Lunch	
1 serving of baked lean meat	1 serving of chicken
Spinach or *saag*	Fenugreek leaves with carrots
A cup of skimmed milk curd	½ cup curd with grated cucumber
1 cup of thin pulses	1 cup of Bengal gram pulse
Raw salad	Raw salad
A guava	A green apple
Dinner	
Clear chicken soup with noodles	Clear soup with sliced mushroom
	Mixed baked vegetables/ sprouts
A toast or a chapati	A chapati or a toast
Iced Fresh fruits	Fruit custard (non-fat) with artificial sweetener

Special Instructions

a) Eat only small portions of allowed foods. For example, eat a small apple instead of a big one.

b) Avoid all trimmings. Mayonnaise, oily salad dressings, kinds of gravy and sauces, for example, are all very high in calories, frequently higher than the main ingredient of the dish.

c) No in-between meal snacks. If unavoidable, due to excessive hunger, snacks should consist of fresh raw vegetables, such as cucumber, carrots, cabbage. These are all very low in calories and all supply a considerable amount of roughage.

Menus for Weight Reduction

A variety of simple but nutritious packed lunches of about 400 cals calories are given below for calorie-conscious people.

Table 5.4 : Menus for Packed Lunches

	Item	*Amounts*
1.	**Noodles with Vegetable and Cottage Cheese**	
	Noodles	60 gm
	Cottage cheese (non-fat)	20 gm
	Vegetable (carrot, cabbage, capsicum, etc)	as per choice
	Oil	a tsp
2.	**Tomato Sandwiches and Bean Sprouts**	
	Sandwiches	bread, two slices
	Tomato	20 gm
	Butter	5 gm
	Bean sprouts	30 gm
	Vegetables (carrot, cabbage, onion, etc)	100 gm
	Lemon	1
3.	**Flaked Rice with Peas and Curd**	
	Flaked Rice (*poha*)	60 gm
	Vegetables (onion, peas, carrot)	150 gm
	Oil	5 gm
	Skimmed-milk curd	75 gm
	Cucumber	50 gm
4.	**Gram Flour Dosa with Coriander Chutney**	
	Dosa	
	Gram flour (*besan*)	60 gm
	Vegetable (onion, green chilli, etc)	20 gm

	Seasoning	to taste
	Coriander chutney	100 gm
	Garlic/onion	50 gm
Note:	*Use a non-stick pan*	
5.	**Semolina Dosa with Coconut Chutney**	
	Dosa	
	Semolina(*suji*)	60 gm
	Refined flour (*maida*)	10 gm
	Curd (non-fat)	30 gm
	Asafoetida (*hing*)	a pinch
	Coconut chutney	
	Coconut	50 gm
	Curd (non-fat)	20 gm
	Roasted channa	10 gm
	Salt and seasoning	to taste
6.	**Rava Idli with Coriander Chutney**	
	Semolina (*suji*)	60 gm
	Bengal gram pulse	10 gm
	Curd (non-fat)	100 gm
	Sodium bicarbonate (*meetha* soda)	a pinch
	Coriander Chutney 100	gm
	Lemon	100 gm
7.	**Soya Dhokla with Curd`**	
	Bengal gram flour	20 gm
	Soya flour	50 gm
	Soya curd	a tbsp
	Eno Fruit Salt	a pinch
	Curry leaves	to taste
	Mustard seeds	few
	Ginger paste	to taste
	Oil	5 gm
	Curd (non-fat)	100g m
8.	**Missi Roti with Curd**	
	Roti	60 gm
	Black gram flour	20 gm
	Fenugreek (*methi*) leaves	75 gm
	Onion	20 gm
	Oil	5 gm
	Curd made from skimmed milk	100 gm
9.	**Nutrella and Peas with Raw Salad**	
	Nutrella nuggets	50 gm
	Fresh peas	50 gm
	Onion/tomatoes	5 gm
	Lemon	1
	Oil	5 gm
	Salad (cucumber, cabbage, carrot, radish)	50 gm

10.	**Chicken Sandwich and Fresh Vegetables**	
	Wholewheat bread	2 slices
	Boiled chicken pieces	30 gm
	White butter	20 gm
	Cabbage	50 gm
	Capsicum	50 gm
11.	**Semolina Upama with Fresh Vegetables**	
	Semolina (*suji*)	60 gm
	Vegetables (carrot, peas, onion, cabbage, capsicum)	150 gm
	Mustard seeds	few
	Salt and seasoning	to taste

Low-Calorie Drinks

In summer one craves for cold aerated drinks. A variety of sweet refreshing and soft drinks are available for a normal person, but a person on a reduction diet needs to be judicious in picking up these thirst quenchers. Here are some low-calorie soft drinks that could be chilled to thrill a calorie-conscious person.

Recipes for Low-Caloric Drinks

		Calories
a)	**Fresh Lime with Soda** Lime juice with iced soda and salt or artificial sweetener. Serve chilled.	10
b)	**Fresh Coconut Water** Green coconut water. Served chilled.	40
c)	**Buttermilk** Well beaten skimmed-milk curd 60 ml, add chilled water and season with salt, pepper or artificial sweetener.	30
d)	**Artificially flavoured Drinks** Make Rasna (artificially flavoured) by adding the flavour in water and mixing with artificial sweetener. Serve chilled.	Nil
e)	**Cold Coffee** Skimmed milk 200 ml Instant coffee Artificial sweetener Shake well and serve chilled.	50
f)	**Jaljeera** Mix readymade Jeera powder with chilled water.	Nil

g) **Fresh Tomato Juice** 50
Make tomato juice of fresh red ripe
tomatoes — 150 ml
Add seasoning and serve chilled.

h) **Fresh Watermelon Juice** 50
Make fresh juice of ripe watermelon — 150 gm
Serve chilled.

i) **Raw Mango Drink** 30
Boil raw mango — 150 gm
Remove skin, mash the pulp in a blender.
Add artificial sweetener and add seasoning as per choice. Serve chilled.

j) **Iced Lemon Tea** Nil
Brew a cup of tea. Squeeze lemon into it but do not add milk.
Chill as per season. Add artificial sweetener.

k) **Thandai** 50
Add a teaspoon of readymade 'Thandai'.
Add artificial sweetener to a glass of water.
Serve chilled.

l) **Flavoured Milk** 50
Skimmed milk — 150 ml
Add rose essence or any other desired flavour.
Add artificial sweetener and serve chilled.

Snacks and Desserts

Nutritious and low calorie snacks and desserts to be taken in-between meals.

	Calories
1. Fresh Fruits and Vegetable Salad	
Apple	25
Guava	25
Cucumber	25
Carrots	20
Lemon	10
Tomato	10

Method: Cut fruits and vegetables in small pieces. Sprinkle 'chaat' masala and lemon to taste.

2. Roti Chaat 70
1 missi roti
Curd, onion, pudina chutney, poppy seeds coriander leaves and chillies.
Seasoning, salt
Oil (1 teaspoon)

Method: Crackle poppy seed in hot oil. Add pudina chutney, onion, seasoning and salt. Crumble missi roti and add to it. Lastly mix it in whipped curd. Garnish with coriander and chillies.

3. **Bean Sprouts** 70

Bean sprouts - 1 cup
Onion - 50 gm
Tomato - 50 gm
Green chillies, lemon
Salt and seasoning

Method: Sprout the beans. Mix all the ingredients and serve.

4. **Bengal gram Chaat** 70

Bengal gram - 20 gm
Onion - 20 gm
Tomato - 20 gm
Coriander leaves, green chillies, lemon
Salt and seasoning

Method: Boil the black gram. Add finely chopped onion and tomato. Garnish with coriander leaves. Add the seasoning and lemon.

5. **Cheese Delight** 80

Cottage cheese - 15 gm
Tomato - 50 gm
Cucumber - 50 gm
Curd - 10 gm
Salt and black pepper

Method: Grate the cucumber and mix it with cottage cheese and curd. Add salt. Cut the tomato into small pieces and sprinkle it on cheese mixture.

6. **Vegetable Noodles** 70

Cabbage - 50 gm
Capsicum - 50 gm
Onion - 20 gm
Beans - 20 gm
Seasoning to taste
Soya sauce and tomato sauce - 1 tablespoon

Method: Cut all the vegetables lengthwise and steam them. Add sauce. Boil the noodles and add to it.

7. **Chickpeas Chaat** 70

Chickpeas - 75 gm
Green chillies - as per paste
Onion - 70 gm
Carrot - 70 gm

Cucumber - 70 gm
Cabbage - 70 gm
Salt and lemon juice - to taste

Method: Boil the chickpeas. Mix all the vegetables after chopping. Add the seasoning and lemon juice.

8. Bottlegourd Kheer 50

Bottlegourd - 100 gm
Skimmed milk - 100 ml
Cardamom - 1 small
Artificial sweetener

Method: Grate the bottlegourd and boil in skimmed milk. Add the cardamom and artificial sweetener after cooling.

9. Snowball 40

Skimmed milk - 200 gm
Egg (white) - 1
Custard powder - 1 teaspoon
Vanilla essence - a drop
Artificial sweetener

Method: Mix the custard powder with cold milk. Cook on a slow fire and stir. Beat the egg white well and add it to the custard with a spoon. Cook for a few minutes. Remove from fire and let it cool. Add the artificial sweetener and essence and serve it chilled or hot.

10. Semolina Kheer 60

Semolina - 50 gm
Skimmed milk - 100 ml
Fat - 5 gm
Artificial sweetener

Method: Roast the semolina in a nonstick pan. Then add fat and put in the roasted semolina. Add an artificial sweetener to water and mix it in semolina. Pour in the milk and stir. Serve hot or cold.

11. Apple Stew 50

Apple, green - 100 gm
Artificial sweetener

Method: Wash and cut the apples into small pieces. Boil the water and add the apple pieces. Remove from the fire and let it cool. Add an artificial sweetener and serve chilled or hot.

12. Shrikhand 100

Curd - 200 ml
Cardamom and nutmeg powder - a pinch
Saffron - a strand
Milk - 2 teaspoons

Dry fruits - optional
Artificial sweetener - to taste

Method: Tie the curd in a muslin cloth and hang it overnight till all the water is drained out. Blend the curd and artificial sweetener in a blender till smooth. For flavouring add the cardamom and nutmeg powder and saffron dissolved in warm milk. Dry fruits may be added if desired. Cool and serve.

13. Chilled Mocha Pudding 70

Skimmed milk - 150 gm, a cup
Coffee powder - 1 teaspoon, 5 gm
Cocoa - ¼ teaspoon
Gelatin - 5 gm
Artificial sweetener - to taste

Method: Boil the milk, add coffee and cocoa. Cool and add the artificial sweetener. Soak the gelatin in 3 tablespoons of water and dissolve on a low flame. Pour the hot gelatin into the milk mixture. Leave to set in the refrigerator.

14. Royal Carrot Pudding 120

Carrots - 50 gm
Milk - 300 ml, 2 cups
Artificial sweetener - to taste

Method: Wash and grate the carrots. Boil in milk till thick. Remove from the fire, cool and add the artificial sweetener.

15. Apple Caramel Compote 80

Apples - 75 gm
Orange sections - 50 gm
Grated orange rind - ½ teaspoon
Water - 1 cup, 150 ml
Sugar - ½ teaspoon
Artificial sweetener - to taste

Method: Caramelise the sugar and add ½ cup warm water to it. Boil the orange rind in water, cool and add the artificial sweetener. Peel and core the apples and cut them into slices. Boil the apple slices in syrup till soft.

16. Jelly Pavlova 30

Pineapple jelly crystals - 10 gm
Milk - 150 ml or one cup
Water - ¼ cup

Method: Mix the jelly crystals in ¼ cup of water. Boil the milk till thick and pour it into the dissolved crystals and allow it to set. Unmould on a plate and sprinkle biscuit crumbs on top if desired.

17. Fruit Summer Cloud 100

Apple - 100 gm
Sapota - 50 gm, 1 medium
Orange juice - 35 ml or ¼ cup

Method: Wash and cut the apples and sapota into 1" pieces and put in the freezer, to let the mixture freeze solid. Before serving, puree the fruits in a blender, add orange juice and serve

18. Fruit Glory 100

Watermelon/papaya/pineapple - 100gm

Method: Cut the fruit and blend into a smooth pulp. Put in an ice tray and freeze. Serve ice-cold.

19. Harvest Caramel Pudding 110

Milk skimmed - 300 ml or a cup
Cornflour - 1 teaspoon
Cocoa powder - 1 teaspoon
Gelatin - 1 teaspoon
Cherries, artificial sweetener - to taste

Method: Boil the milk add cornflour, mix with a little water into a smooth paste and cook till it is slightly thick. Add cocoa powder, cool and add artificial sweetener. In ¼ cup of water add gelatin and let it stand for 5 minutes. Heat the gelatin on a very low flame. Pour it into the milk mixture. Pour the whole mixture in the pudding bowl and set in the refrigerator. Serve cold.

20. Orange Delight 120

Orange juice - 2 tablespoons
Lemon juice - 1 teaspoon
Egg - 1
Artificial sweetener - to taste
Gelatin - 1 teaspoon
Salt - a pinch
Orange essence - a drop
Cherries/currants - optional

Method: Separate the egg yolk and the white. Whisk the lemon juice, orange juice, salt and egg yolk with a beater. Cook in a double boiler for 5 to 7 minutes. Add the soaked gelatin and continue cooking till the gelatin is dissolved. Cool and add the artificial sweetener. Beat the egg white stiff and fold into the mixture. Grease a bowl or line it with butter paper and pour the mixture into it. Put in the refrigerator to set. Unmould and decorate as desired.

Fat-Free Recipes

1. **Scrambled Egg White** 80
   Egg white - 2
   Water - 30 ml
   Yellow food colour - a drop
   Salt and pepper

Method: Whisk the egg white with water. Add colouring. Place in a nonstick pan/bowl over boiling water. Cook slowly, stirring all the time until set. A little mustard or tomato ketchup may be added if desired.

2. **Broad Beans in Tomato Sauce** 50
   Broad beans - 40 gm
   Onion - 1
   Tomato puree - 1 tablespoon
   Water - 50 ml
   Salt, pepper, sugar

Method: Chop the onion and cook with a little water in a non-stick pan over gentle heat, and stir till soft. Add shelled broad beans, seasonings, tomato puree and water. Simmer gently with lid on till the beans are tender. Remove the lid and simmer a few minutes to reduce liquid to a syrupy consistency. Check seasoning and serve.

3. **Dhokla** 80
   Gram flour (besan) - 20 gm
   Curd (non-fat) - 50 ml
   Eno salt - a pinch
   Salt and seasoning - to taste

Method: Beat the curd, mix in gram flour and stir. Add Eno Salt and seasoning and steam in a pressure cooker for 10 minutes without putting on the whistle. Serve with coriander chutney.

4. **Rava Idli** 80
   Rava (semolina) - 20 gm
   Curd (non-fat) - 50 ml
   Eno Salt - a pinch
   Salt and seasoning - to taste

Method: Same as for Dhokla.

5. **Low-Fat Biscuits** 80
   Plain flour (maida) - 50 gm
   Ground rice - 10 gm
   Baking powder - ¼ teaspoons
   Sugar - 15 gm

Water - 2 tablespoons
Caramel syrup - 1 tablespoon

Method: Add sufficient water and syrup to the flour to bind into a dough. Roll out and cut into rounds. Bake in a moderately hot oven for 10 mins.

Note: Caramel syrup is made by heating sugar in a nonstick pan. When it gets brown add a cup of water and let it boil. Remove from the fire and store in a bottle in a refrigerator.

6. Angel Cake (fat-free) 110

Egg white - 20
Maida - 40 gm
Castor sugar - 25 gm
Flavouring and colouring

Method: Whisk the egg white until stiff. Add the sugar and flavouring, fold in the sieved flour. Divide into three parts and pour equal amounts of the mixture into three tins. Colour each mixture differently. Bake for 10–15 minutes in a moderate oven. Turn out each cake, one on top of the other in layers and serve.

Note: It is best eaten on the day it is cooked.

7. Fruit Bun (fat-free)

Plain flour - 40 gm 100
Salt - a pinch
Dried yeast - 2 gm
Warm water - 30 ml
Dry fruit (Mixed) - 20 gm
Sugar - 10 gm

Method: Mix the water, sugar and yeast together and leave in a warm place for 10-15 minutes until the mixture becomes frothy. Mix the dry ingredients together in the yeast mixture. Knead well. Place the dough in a warm place for about an hour until the dough has doubled in size. Shape into small buns and leave to rise for 15 minutes on a warm tray. Bake in a hot oven for 10–15 minutes. Mix some sugar and water and glaze the buns immediately, as soon as they are taken out of the oven.

8. Fat-free Pastry 120

Plain flour - 50 gm
Baking powder - ¼ teaspoon
Salt - a pinch
Egg white - 1
Water

Method: Mix together the sieved flour, baking powder and salt. Mix in the egg white and add enough water to form a soft dough. Roll out in the usual manner. Bake in a hot oven for about 20 minutes.

9. Ice-cream (low fat) 210

Non-fat milk powder - 30 gm
Water - 230 ml
Sugar - 30 gm
Cornflour - 15 gm
Egg whites - 2
Flavouring and colouring

Method: Place the non-fat milk powder, sugar, cornflour, flavouring and water in a pan and cook, stirring the whole time. Whisk the egg whites until stiff and fold into the mixture. Freeze.

10. Sandwich Fillings 80

Cottage cheese fillings
Use cottage cheese as a meat substitute
Mix with cucumber, pineapple, lettuce, tomato sliced and radishes, parsley, mint, celery and marmite chopped.

Foods to Be Strictly Avoided

Each Given Portion Provides 100 Calories

Rasgulla (squeezed)	30 gm
Gulab jamun	25 gm
Jalebi	30 gm
Burfi	25 gm
Besan ka ladoo	25 gm
Chana chiki	20 gm
Suji halwa	25 gm
Gajjar ka halwa	25 gm
Sponge cake	25 gm
Fruit cake	25 gm
Chocolate	25 gm
Bourbon biscuits	25 gm
Orange cream biscuits, 2	20 gm
Vegetable burger	1 gm
Chicken burger	1 gm
Noodles (Maggie)	25 gm
Small samosa	35 gm
Namakpara	15 gm
Sago vada	30 gm
Dal vada	25 gm
Cheese ball	20 gm
Potato chips	15 gm

Fryums	15 gm
Sapota (chiku)	90 gm
Banana	75 gm
Grapes	120 gm
Orange	120 gm
Dates (dried)	25 gm
Coconut (dried)	20 gm
Pista, salted	20 gm
Walnut, shelled	15 gm
Groundnut, salted	18 gm
Almonds	18 gm
Cashewnuts	18 gm
Coconut, fresh	20 gm
Ice-cream (non-fat)	1 serving

Sterling's 30-Day Diet to Lose Weight

Many foods and food substitutes are available to help weight reduction. However, moderation is the key rather than continuing with the same old eating habits. If you wish to lose weight permanently, then the scientific way is to make lifelong changes in your eating habits and exercise. The basic types of food in this category that help weight reduction are the ones made with artificial sweeteners which supply no calories to the body. Other types of such foods contain an appreciable amount of fibre which absorb high quantities of water. The fibre gives the stomach the sensation of being full and thus decreases the appetite. It is this psychological factor that gives a person the feeling of satisfaction and helps to increase his ability to stay on a diet. Food high in oils (and high in calories) can be moderated by using water during preparation or by changing the method of cooking, such as steaming instead of frying food.

All these methods will work only if the total intake of calories is reduced. Overeating, even of low calorie food is a taboo. The primary principle therefore is *to reduce calorie intake and increase calorie expenditure or preferably, do both.* Learning how to keep weight off through a maintenance programme is just as important as losing weight. Serious commitment to a diet programme helps to maintain sensible eating habits.

Food Plans

Many of these food plans are diets ranging from 1,000 to 1,500 calories a day, where weight loss is likely to average ½ to 1 kg a week. You need to follow a carefully controlled menu plan. By and large, the more slowly you lose weight and the longer you maintain that weight loss, the safer that diet is for you. It is particularly important for those with diabetes, high blood pressure, heart disease or gallbladder disease to check the diet plan with their physician for his approval. Parents may like to check the diet programmc of thcir children. Pregnant women are advised not to follow a diet programme.

Sterling's 30-Day Weight-Watcher's Slim Fast Diet

Day 1

Time	*Menu*	*Quantity*	*Calories*
Early morning	Tea/Coffee	1 cup	20
	Artificial sweetener		
Breakfast	A scrambled egg		80
	A slice of brown bread		70
	Skimmed milk	1 cup	50
Lunch	Spinach	150–200 gm	100
	Bengal gram dal	15 gm	
	with gourd	40 gm	60
	Chapatis	2 medium	140
	Cucumber in curd	1½cup	60
	Raw salad	as desired	
	Apple	1 small	50
Evening snacks	Tea with artificial sweetener	1 cup	20
	2 cream cracker biscuits		20
Dinner	Thin vegetable soup	150 ml/1 cup	50
	Baked mixed vegetables	180–200 gm	200
	Soya bean curry	30 gm	200
	(Soya bean nuggets)		
	Plain curd	1 cup	50
	Dessert - Snowball	1 cup	40
	Total		1,210

Day 2

Time	*Menu*	*Quantity*	*Calories*
Early morning	Fresh lime and salt	1 glass	Nil
Breakfast	Skimmed milk	150 ml, 1 cup	50
	Cornflakes	30 gm	
Lunch	Sprouted green gram	45 gm	210
	Chapatis	40 gm, 2 medium	140
	Raw salad	as desired	
	Pear	1 (small)	50
Evening snacks	Cucumber sandwich	2 medium	100
	Tea or coffee	1 cup	20
Dinner	Soya soup	1 cup	100
	Dal	1 cup	120
	Cauliflower and tomato	200 gm, 1 cup	150
	Plain boiled rice	15 gm, $^1/_3$ cup	50
	Chapatis	40 gm, 2 medium	140
	Plain curd	1 cup	50
	Raw salad	as desired	—
	Semolina kheer	15 gm, ½ cup	60
	Total		1,240

Note:

1) Skimmed milk is used in all preparations.
2) Artificial sweetener is taken instead of sugar.
3) Rice is boiled and then strained to remove the starch.

Day 3

Time	*Menu*	*Quantity*	*Calories*
Early morning	Warm water and lime juice	1 glass	Nil
Breakfast	Cold skimmed milk	150 ml, 1 cup	50
	Scrambled egg	1	120
	Bread	1 slice	70
Lunch	Dal	15 gm, ½ cup	60
	Spinach with meat	200 gm + 10 gm	150
	Plain curd	1 cup	50
	Chapatis	40 gm, 2	140
	Raw salad	as desired	—
	Orange	1 small	60

Snacks	Flaked rice and peas	20 gm	70
Dinner	Vegetable noodles	20 gm	70
	Tomato soup	1 cup	50
	Total		890

Day 4

Time	*Menu*	*Quantity*	*Calories*
Early morning	Tea/coffee	1 cup	20
Breakfast	Cold coffee	1 cup	50
	Bengal gram chaat	20 gm	70
Mid-morning	Fresh coconut water	1	40
Lunch	Semolina dosa with coconut chutney	60 gm, 3	400
	Fruit	1	100
Dinner	Thin vegetable soup	1 cup	50
	Baked mixed vegetable	1 cup	100
	Bread	1 slice	70
	Fruit	1	100
	Total		1,000

Day 5

Time	*Menu*	*Quantity*	*Calories*
Early morning	Tea		20
Breakfast	Missi roti with mint chutney	1, medium	70
	Buttermilk	1 glass	30
Lunch	Baked fish with tomato	30 gm	225
	Dal with spinach	15 gm, 100 gm	90
	Plain curd	50 ml	50
	Chapatis	3, medium	210
	Raw salad		
Evening	Fresh lime with soda	1 glass	Nil
	Marie biscuits	2	50
Dinner	Baked chicken with vegetables	15 gm, 70 gm	120
	Thin chicken soup	1 cup	100
	Bread	1 slice	70
	Jelly pavlova	½ cup	30
	Total		1,065

Day 6

Time	*Menu*	*Quantity*	*Calories*
Early morning	Tea or fresh lime water	20	Nil
Breakfast	Idli with sambhar	2, 30 gm	150
	Milk	1 cup	70
Lunch	Noodles with	60 gm	400
	vegetables and	100 gm	
	cottage cheese (non-fat)	20 gm	
Snacks	Chilled tomato juice	1 cup	50
	Dhokla	25 gm	150
Dinner	Chicken soup	1 cup	130
	Chicken sandwich, crisp	2	110
	Harvest caramel pudding	1 cup	110
	Total		1,170

Day 7

Time	*Menu*	*Quantity*	*Calories*
Early morning	Fresh lime water		Nil
Breakfast	Fruit juice	1 cup	100
	Egg omelette with cheese	1 egg, 20 gm	200
Lunch	Sprouted black gram with raw vegetables	40 gm	140
	Fresh fruit	1, small	50
Dinner	Clear soup with sliced mushroom	1 cup	100
	Dal	1 katori, 30 gm	70
	Methi with carrot	1 katori, 200 gm	100
	Chapatis	2, medium	140
	Fruit glory	1 cup	100
	Total		1,000

Day 8

Time	*Menu*	*Quantity*	*Calories*
Early Morning	Lemon with water	1 cup	Nil
Breakfast	Flavoured milk	1 cup	50
	Papaya	200 gm	70
Mid-morning	Buttermilk	1 cup	30
Lunch	Spinach soup	1 cup	50
	Soft khichdi with ghee	30 gm	100
	Plain curd	1 cup	50
Evening	Tea or coffee with		
	Rava idli	1 cup, 1	70
Dinner	Clear chicken soup	1 cup	110
	Thin boiled dal	30 gm	100
	Lauki (bottlegourd)	70 gm	100
	Apple stew	1 cup	50
	Chapatis	2, medium	140
	Milk	1 glass	80
	Total		1,000

Day 9

Time	*Menu*	*Quantity*	*Calories*
Early Morning	Fresh lime/sweetener	1 cup	20
Breakfast	Boiled egg	1	85
	Brown bread	2	50
	Milk	1 cup	50
Lunch	Flaked rice with peas cooked in oil	60 gm	400
	Cucumber with curd	50 gm	50
Evening	Cold coffee	1 cup	50
Dinner	Tomato soup	1 cup	50
	Thin dal	15 gm	50
	French beans	100 gm	100
	Chapati	1 small	50
	Rice	15 gm	50
	Curd	1 cup	50
	Raw salad	–	
	Fresh summer cloud pudding	1 serving	100
	Total		1,155

Day 10

Time	*Menu*	*Quantity*	*Calories*
Early Morning	Fresh lime water		Nil
Breakfast	Soya cheela with	2, medium	100
	curd	1 cup	50
	Jaljeera	1 cup	Nil
Lunch	Chicken sandwich	2,30 gm	
	Raw vegetables	50 gm	300
	Fresh fruit	1 small	
Snacks	Rasna drink	1 glass	50
	Bran biscuit	2	20
Dinner	Classic fish soup	1 cup	100
	Thin dal	½ cup	50
	Fresh peas with		
	tomato	30 gm	100
	Chapatis	2, medium	140
	Curd	1 cup	50
	Fruit	1, small	50
	Total		1,010

Day 11

Time	*Menu*	*Quantity*	*Calories*
Early Morning	Fresh lime water	1 cup	Nil
Breakfast	Vegetable and		
	mushroom sand-	2 slice	200
	wich Cheese	20 gm	80
Lunch	Thin dal with bottle-		
	gourd	15 gm, 70 gm	100
	Capsicum with onion	1 cup	100
	Curd	1 cup	50
	Chapatis	2, medium	140
	Raw salad	as desired	—
Evening	Small fruit	1	50
Dinner	Noodles with		
	vegetables	50 gm	200
	Thin soup	1 cup	100
	Ice-cream (low fat)	1 cup	70
	Total		1,090

Day 12

Time	*Menu*	*Quantity*	*Calories*
Early Morning	Fresh lime water		Nil
Breakfast	Roti chat with chutney	1 cup	70
	Orange juice	1 cup	100
Lunch	Missi roti	3, medium	400
	Curd	1 cup	
Evening	Angel cake (fat-free)	1, small	110
Dinner	Thin soup	1 cup	50
	Spinach with cottage cheese	100 gm, 20 gm	150
	Thin dal	1 cup	70
	Chapatis	2, medium	140
	Orange delight pudding	1 cup	110
	Total		1,200

Day 13

Time	*Menu*	*Quantity*	*Calories*
Early Morning	Fresh lime water/ Tea/Coffee	1 cup	Nil/20
Breakfast	Boiled egg	1	80
	Brown bread	2	50
	Milk	1 cup	50
Lunch	Stuffed capsicum with meat	2 15 gm	160
	Chapatis	2, medium	140
	Fruit	1, small	50
Snacks	Tea/sweetener	1 cup	20
	Fat-free Angel cake	1, small	100
Dinner	Thin soup	1 cup	50
	Amaranth saag	1 cup	50
	Dal	1 cup, 30 gm	100
	Salad		
	Chapatis	2, medium	140
	Total		990

Day 14

Time	*Menu*	*Quantity*	*Calories*
Early Morning	Fresh lime water	1 cup	Nil
Breakfast	Semolina upama with chutney	30 gm	200
	Jaljeera	1 cup	Nil
Lunch	Soya bean chunks (Nutrella)	20 gm	150
	Bottlegourd with tomato	1 cup	100
	Curd	1 cup	50
	Chapatis	2, small	100
	Raw salad		
Snacks	Fruit	1, small	50
Dinner	Fat-free burger (vegetable)	1 small	300
	Shrikhand	1 cup	110
	Total		1,060

Day 15

Time	*Menu*	*Quantity*	*Calories*
Early Morning	Fresh lime water	1 cup	Nil
Breakfast	Dhokla with chutney	4 pieces, 40 gm	200
	Iced lemon tea	1 cup	Nil
Lunch	Sambhar dal	1 cup	150
	Lady's finger with onion	1 cup	100
	Curd	1 cup	50
	Raw salad	—	—
	Chapati	1	70
	Rice	½ katori	150
Dinner	Sprouts with fresh vegetable	1 cup	120
	Raw salad		
	Shahi carrot kheer	1 cup	120
	Chapati/bread	1	70
	Milk	1 cup	70
	Total		1,100

Day 16

Time	*Menu*	*Quantity*	*Calories*
Early Morning	Fresh lime water	1 cup	Nil
Breakfast	Vegetable sandwich with 1 teaspoon white butter	2	200
Lunch	Soya bean, nuggets and peas with raw salad	60 gm	400
Evening	Jaljeera	1 cup	Nil
	Fruit	1, small	50
Dinner	Chicken broth	1 cup	100
	Chicken with capsicum	1 cup	200
	Yogurt	1 cup	50
	Thin dal	1 cup	50
	Chapatis	2	140
	Total		1,190

Day 17

Time	*Menu*	*Quantity*	*Calories*
Early morning	Fresh lime with honey	1 cup	Nil
Breakfast	Noodles with capsicum	50 gm, 30 gm	200
	Milk	1 cup	50
Lunch	Mixed vegetable sambhar	1½ cup	180
	Boiled rice	20 gm	100
	Curd	1 cup	50
	Fresh fruit	1, small	50
Snacks	Soya bean kabab	2	100
	Tea/coffee	1 cup	20
Dinner	Thin soup	1 cup	50
	Scrambled egg	1	120
	Bread	2 slices	140
	Milk	1 cup	50
	Total		1,110

Day 18

Time	*Menu*	*Quantity*	*Calories*
Early Morning	Fresh lime water with salt	1 cup	Nil
Breakfast	Rava dosa (cooked in low fat)	2	260
	Sambhar	1 cup	100
Lunch	Missi roti	2	140
	Curd	1 cup	50
	Vegetable cutlet	1	70
Evening	Tea with biscuit	1	20
Dinner	Thin vegetable soup	1 cup	50
	Baked mixed vegetables with cheese	1 serving	100
	Boiled chicken with capsicum	1 serving	130
	Bread	2 slices	140
	Ice-cream/caramel pudding	1 serving	110
	Total		1,170

Day 19

Time	*Menu*	*Quantity*	*Calories*
Early Morning	Fresh lime water with honey	1 cup	Nil
Breakfast	Grilled bread (2) with vegetables (baked)	50 gm	170
	Sauce	10 gm	20
	Milk	1 cup	50
Lunch	Meat curry	1 katori	200
	Brinjal with tomato	1 katori	120
	Curd	1 katori	50
	Raw salad		
	Chapatis	2	140
Snack	Fruit	1, small	50
Dinner	Thin dal	15 gm	50
	Mixed vegetables	1 katori	100
	Raw salad		
	Rice	1 katori	100
	Rajkeera kheer	½ cup	120
	Total		1,170

Day 20

Time	*Menu*	*Quantity*	*Calories*
Early Morning	Fresh lime	1 cup	Nil
Breakfast	Boiled chana with lime	1 katori	80
	Milk	1 glass	50
Lunch	Thin dal	1 katori	100
	Spinach with cottage cheese	1 serving	120
	Curd	1 cup	50
	Raw salad	—	—
	Rice, chapatis	1 cup, 2	170
Evening	Tomato juice	1 glass	50
Dinner	Thin soup	1 cup	50
	Sprouts with chutney	1 katori	120
	Caramel custard	1 cup	100
	Total		890

Day 21

Time	*Menu*	*Quantity*	*Calories*
Early Morning	Tea/coffee		Nil
Breakfast	Chapatis with (fenugreek leaves)	2, small	140
	Curd	1 katori	50
Lunch	Dal with spinach	30 gm, 40 gm	200
	Meat curry	15 gm	150
	Boiled rice	15 gm	50
	Chapatis	2	140
	Plain curd	1 cup	50
	Raw salad	—	—
Snacks	Tomato juice	1 cup	50
	Fruit bun (fat-free)	1	100
Dinner	Mixed vegetables with noodles	50 gm	200
	Soup	1 cup	50
	Snowball pudding	1 serving	40
	Total		1,220

Day 22

Time	*Menu*	*Quantity*	*Calories*
Early Morning	Tea/coffee		Nil
Breakfast	Boiled egg	1	70
	Cottage cheese	20 gm	80
	Milk	1 cup	50
Lunch (packed)	Semolina upama	60 gm	300
	Fresh fruit	1	50
Snacks	Mushroom and vegetable sandwich	2	200
	Tea	1 cup	20
Dinner	Thin dal	1 katori	50
	Cabbage with tomato	1 katori	100
	Curd	1 cup	50
	Chapati	1	70
	Total		1,040

Day 23

Time	*Menu*	*Quantity*	*Calories*
Early Morning	Fresh lime		Nil
Breakfast	Skimmed milk porridge (Dalia)	1 cup, 30 gm	150
Mid-morning	Bran biscuit	2	50
	Apple	1	50
Lunch (packed)	Sprouted green gram	45 gm	200
	Chapati	1	70
	Salad	—	—
Evening	Orange juice	1 glass	100
Dinner	Cauliflower with tomato	20 gm	100
	Thin dal	20 gm	110
	Curd	1 cup	50
	Chapatis	2	140
	Total		1,020

Day 24

Time	*Menu*	*Quantity*	*Calories*
Early Morning	Milk	1 cup	50
	Marie biscuits	3	75
Breakfast	Boiled egg	1	85
	Brown bread	2 slices	50
Mid-morning	Grilled fish	1 piece	50
Lunch	Bengal gram with fenugreek roti	2, small	140
	Apple	1	50
Evening	Spongy delight	30 gm	150
Dinner	Tomato soup	1 cup	50
	Rice	15 gm	50
	Dal	30 gm	155
	French beans	150 gm	115
	Chapati	1, small	50
	Fruit summer cloud	1 serving	100
	Total		1,170

Day 25

Time	*Menu*	*Quantity*	*Calories*
Early morning	Tea/coffee without sugar	1 cup	20
Breakfast	Skimmed milk with	1 cup	50
	cornflakes	30 gm	100
Packed lunch	Sprouted green gram	45 gm, 1½ cup	210
	Chapatis 3 medium,	60 gm	210
	Salad	—	—
Evening	Tea	1 cup	20
	Biscuits	2	40
Dinner	Soya soup	1 cup	150
	Tomato with cauliflower	200 gm, 1 cup	150
	Black gram dal with vegetables	20 gm, 1 cup	130
	Plain rice	15 gm, ½ cup	50
	Chapatis	40 gm, 2 medium	140
	Salad	—	—
	Total		1,270

Day 26

Time	*Menu*	*Quantity*	*Calories*
Early Morning	Lime juice		
	Light tea without sugar	Nil	
Breakfast	Cold skimmed milk	150 ml, 1 cup	50
	Scrambled egg	1	120
	Brown bread	2, medium	50
Lunch	Spinach	150–200 gm	60
	Dal with tinda	15 gm, ½ cup	60
	Chapatis	2, medium	140
	Cucumber in curd	1 ½ cups	60
Evening	Marie biscuits	2	50
	Buttermilk	1 glass	30
Dinner	French beans with meat	200 gm, 1 cup	150
	Dal	15 gm, ½ cup	60
	Chapatis	2, medium	140
	Plain curd	1 cup	50
	Cold milk	1 cup	50
	Total		1,070

Day 27

Time	*Menu*	*Quantity*	*Calories*
Early Morning	Light tea/coffee	150 ml	20
Breakfast	Semolina kheer	1 cup	100
	Papaya	150–200 gm	70
Mid-morning	Buttermilk	210 ml	30
	Salted biscuits	2	50
Lunch	Spinach soup	1 cup	50
	Khichdi without fat	30 gm	100
	Plain curd	150 ml	50
Evening	Tea/coffee	150 ml	20
	Marie biscuits	3	75
	Stewed pear	100–150 gm	70
Dinner	Clear chicken and vegetable soup	150 ml	110
	Thin dal	30 gm	100
	Plain rice	15 gm	50
	Dalia Porridge with milk	150 ml	210
	Total		1,105

Day 28

Time	*Menu*	*Quantity*	*Calories*
Early Morning	Fresh lime water		Nil
Breakfast	Salted biscuits	2	50
	Rava idli with coriander chutney	25 gm	150
	Skimmed milk without sugar/soya milk	150 ml	50
Lunch	Dal with bottlegourd	25 gm, 1 cup	120
	Baked vegetables	220 gm	150
	Chapatis	2, medium	140
	Soya curd with onion and tomatoes	1 cup, 150 ml	60
Evening	Tea with biscuits		20
Dinner	Fish curry	25 gm	165
	Capsicum	200 gm	150
	Rice	15 gm	50
	Chapati	1, medium	70
	Raw salad with lemon dressing		
	Total		1,150

Day 29

Time	*Menu*	*Quantity*	*Calories*
Early Morning	Tea	1 cup	Nil
Breakfast	Scrambled eggs	1 egg	120
	Brown bread	4 slices	100
	Orange juice	75 ml, ½ cup	90
Lunch	Stuffed capsicum	150–200 gm	160
	Chapatis	2, medium	140
Evening	Idli with	2	100
	sambhar	30 gm	150
Dinner	Baked fish with tomato rings	30 gm	225
	Noodles	40 gm	140
	Chilled mocha pudding	1 serving	70
	Total		1,295

Day 30

Time	*Menu*	*Quantity*	*Calories*
Early Morning	Tea with lime, salted biscuits	2	100
Breakfast	Rava dosa	45 gm; 2, small	260
	Buttermilk	210 ml, 1 glass	30
Mid-morning	Fruit	1 medium	70
Lunch	Bottlegourd with tomatoes	150–200 gm	125
	Dal/ 1 egg / meat/ cottage cheese	30 gm	150
	Chapatis	2, medium	140
	Raw salad		
Evening	Yoghurt	150 ml	20
Dinner	Thin soup		
	Amaranth saag	150–200 gm	160
	Chapatis	2, medium	140
	Rice with vegetables	15 gm	130
	Raw salad	—	—
	Chilled stewed apple	1 cup	50
	Total		1,375

Note: Recipes for various food preparations given in the Sterling's 30 day diet, are mentioned in the chapter 17 of the book 'Speaking of Diabetes and Diet', published by Sterling Publishers.

UNIT VI

HEALTH AND NUTRITION

INTRODUCTION

Eating is something we do everyday — something that can either build and maintain our health or seriously undermine it. Eating well requires that one knows about nutrition so as to appropriately choose nourishing foods and accordingly prepare them to retain these nutrients. There is a general agreement among nutritionists that most serious abnormal physiological conditions can be improved by proper diet modifications. For example, whatever the reason for high blood cholesterol level, the immediate treatment prescribed by the doctor is 'diet control'. If the blood cholesterol level does not decrease sufficiently with the right diet, then your doctor may consider adding cholesterol-lowering medications to your dietary treatment. Medicines are meant to supplement and not replace a low saturated fat/ low cholesterol diet. The relation between diet and health has increased the awareness for 'healthier eating'.

It should be remembered that dietary foods are foods and not medicines. Claims about the curative and preventive properties of some foods often lead to confusion and misunderstanding and they ought to be ignored. The two main categories of dietary foods are:

a) Foods which are designed to meet normal physiological conditions specifically like those suitable for infants or children, adolescents, old age, pregnancy or lactation.

b) Foods which meet the special nutritional needs of people suffering from abnormal physiological conditions such as obesity, diabetes, hypertension, heart problems, etc.

Diet According to Age

Infancy

During the first few days of their life, infants lose weight; but the birth weight is usually regained by the seventh to the tenth day of life. Infants usually double their weight by the fourth month and triple it by the age of one year. They increase their height by 50 per cent during the first year and double it by the fourth year. A newly born infant acquires certain essential elements from the mother's milk, while his own immune system is gaining maturation. Breast-feeding is strongly recommended for babies except where specific contra-indications exist. Ideally, breast milk should be practically the only source of nutrients for the first four to six months for most infants.

Food for Infants

A variety of commercially prepared foods are available for infants. However, many mothers prefer to make their own. Home-prepared foods generally have a higher concentration of nutrients than commercially prepared ones and they are easy to make.

Tips for Homemade Infant Food

a) Select good quality cereals, fruits, vegetables or meat.
b) Ensure that all nutrients are thoroughly cleaned.
c) Wash hands before preparing the food.
d) Cook the food until tender. Put in as little water as possible. Avoid overcooking as it may destroy heat-sensitive nutrients.
e) Strain or puree the food if required.
f) Do not add salt. Add sugar sparingly. Do not add honey for infants of less than one year of age (because honey may have microorganisms called 'botulism spores' which can cause infections that an infant does not have the capacity to fight).

Table 6.1 : Recommended Daily Allowance Chart for Infants

Particulars	*Body wt in kg*	*Net energy cal*	*Protein gm/d*	*Fat gm/d*	*Calcium mg/d*	*Iron mg/d*
0–6months	5.4	118/kg	2.05/kg	-	50	-
6–12months	8.6	102/kg	1.65/kg	-	500	-

Note: *gm/d is gms per day*
mg/d is milligrams per day

g) Cereals like sago *(sabudana)*, custard or semolina can be cooked in milk with a little sugar.
h) Fruit juices and vegetable puree are ideal for children as it meets their vitamin needs appreciably.

Right Foods for Children up to Two Years of Age

a) Cook cereals like sago or semolina in milk with a little sugar.
b) Soft fruits such as bananas, peaches, apple, papaya, etc.
c) Sweet biscuits, cheese, mashed potatoes (foods should be soluble in the mouth to prevent choking).
d) Well cooked rice, dal, cereal, vegetables, peeled ripe fruits.
e) Raw vegetables and fruit should be introduced gradually.

Table 6.2 : When to Begin Juices, Semisolids and Table Foods

	Age in months		
Foods	*4–6*	*6–8*	*9–12*
Cooked cereal for infants like sago, semolina, custard	To be given	Can be continued	Can be continued
Vegetables	-	Strained	Gradually omit strained food and introduce table food.
Fruit	-	Strained	Gradually omit strained food and introduce chopped and well cooked foods.
Meat	-	Strained	Decrease the use of strained meat and increase the variety of table meats.

Foods	Age in months		
	4–6	6–8	9–12
Well cooked, mashed or chopped food without salt or sugar	-	-	Yes
Juice or milk in a cup		-	Yes

Childhood

As children grow and develop teeth, muscles and bones, they need nutritious food in proportion to their weight. They are prone to malnutrition when they have a prolonged poor appetite or accept a limited number of foods only or are sick.

Mothers usually despair about the eating behaviour of pre-school children. The usual complaints are that children eat too many sweets, eat too little of the nutritious homemade meals and prefer junk food or avoid fruits and vegetables. Harassed mothers feel that they drink too many soft drinks, or eat too much non-vegetarian food, etc. This behaviour may be due to the boredom with everyday foods. This is often a difficult time for parents who are unduly concerned about the irrational eating habits of their children and the adequacy of their diet. A parent should understand that this period is temporary and transient. A variety of healthy foods should be offered to children as they usually respond well when offered with a choice, rather than given the same type of food everyday.

Eating Habits

Most children eat 4 to 6 times a day, making snacks as substantial as their meals as far as nutrients are concerned. Their snacks need to be carefully chosen so that they are packed with nutrients and are not limited to calorie-filled snacks like cookies, pastries, soda, ice-cream, chips, etc.

Foods that are likely to cause dental caries should be avoided. Wholesome snacks enjoyed by many young children are fresh fruits, hard-boiled eggs, cheese, vegetable or butter sandwiches, idli, dosa, poha, upama, dhokla and sprouts.

Table 6.3 : Recommended Daily Allowance for Children

Group	*Particulars*	*Body wt/kg*	*Net energy cal*	*Protein gm/d*	*Fat gm/d*	*Calcium mg/d*	*Iron mg/d*
Children	1–3 yrs	12.1	1125	23	20	400	12
	4–6 yrs	18.2	1600	31	20	400	18
	7–9 yrs	25.2	1925	41	20	400	25

Note: gm/d is gms per day
mg/d is milligrams per day

Children will grow and develop the best when they are given adequate nutrition along with an appreciation of his or her own uniqueness. Parents and others working with children need to be understanding about the social and psychological aspects of food and eating, and the individual tastes of a child.

What Pre-school Children should Eat

Here is a guide for the basic diet of small children. Foods can be selected from this pattern for meals and snacks.

Table 6.4 : Diet for Pre-School Children

Foods	*2-3 Years Old*		*4-6 Years Old*	
	Portion size	*No. of serving*	*Portion size*	*No. of serving*
Milk and Dairy Products Curd, buttermilk, yogurt, cheese	½ cup	3–4	½ cup	2–3
Meat, fish, eggs, poultry	30 gm (1 egg)	1–2	30 gm	1–2
Fruits and Vegetables Vegetables include one green leafy or yellow vegetable for vitamin A such as spinach, methi, carrot or pumpkin.				
Cooked	2–3 table-spoons	3–4 table-spoons		
*Raw	A few pieces	A few pieces		
Fruits Include one vitamin C rich fruit or juice, such as citrus juices, orange, grapes, lemon, strawberries, tomatoes.				
Lemon raw	½–1 small		½–1 small	
Lemon juice	½ cup		½–1 cup	

*(*Do not give raw vegetables to children until they can chew well*)

Adolescence

Adolescence is the period of life between childhood and adulthood characterised by a rapid increase in the rate of physical growth. It is the age group of 9.5–13.5 years with an average of 11.5 years for males and 1 to 2 years earlier for females.

Nutritional Counselling for Adolescents

Nutritional counselling generally should take into account the cultural aspects of the family diet and attitude of the teenager towards food. It is far better to give them information about nutrition together with the associated changes than imposing an eating schedule. Information about the normal physical changes of adolescence also helps.

Sports and Nutritional Requirements

The adolescent athlete or sportsman has to pay particular attention to the diet because of the increased calorie demands.

Tips

1) A higher calorie intake in the form of a balanced diet is far better than fast foods which are carbohydrate-rich.
2) Increased protein needs can be met by a diet consisting of foods like meat, poultry, milk, dried fruit, pulses and soya beans.
3) Athletes should avoid a diet including high carbohydrates since sugar is stored in the body for a short period and will not provide energy during prolonged training hours.
4) Salt intake to be restricted to avoid water retention.
5) Anabolic steroids used by some for weight gain and increase of strength are medically unsafe.
6) An adequate intake of iron is particularly important for female adolescents (12 to 28 mg/day).

Table 6.5 : Foods to be included and not to be included for Adolescents

To be Include	*Not to Include*
For Snacks Sprouts, rava dosa, (semolina dosa), rava idli, egg sandwiches, brown bread, chicken sandwiches, dhokla	(Food rich in carbohydrates) Noodles, pizzas, patties, Non-vegetarian or vegetarian burgers
Fresh Juices Lemon water, plain coconut water, homemade drinks from fruits.	Soft drinks
Thin soups	Thick soups with butter
Raw salad	Salads with oil dressing
Fresh fruits	Canned and tinned fruits in syrup
Fresh vegetables	Canned or fried vegetables

Obesity

Obesity is a major nutritional disorder affecting adolescents. Obesity does not spare anyone who overeats. During this period of increasing self-awareness, the adolescent with a poor body image may withdraw from social contact or develop aggressive behaviour problems.

Diet Plan

The 30-day diet plan mentioned earlier can also be followed by adolescents.

Alcoholism

Chronic alcoholism may result in nutritional deprivation, liver disease, heart problems, etc. The effect of alcohol on the growth and hormone balance can be quite profound and may result in permanent damage. Consuming alcohol only increases your calorie intake.

Table 6.6 : Recommended Daily Allowance for Adolescents

Group	*Particulars*	*Body wt/kg*	*Net energy cal*	*Protein g/d*	*Fat g/d*	*Calcium mg/d*	*Iron mg/d*
Boys	10–12 years	33.5	2150	53	15	600	28
Girls	10–12 years	35	1950	55	15	600	20
Boys	13–15 years	46.8	2400	71	15	600	43
Girls	13–15 years	47.8	2050	67	15	600	28
Boys	16–18 years	56.1	2600	79	15	600	50
Girls	16–18 years	49.7	2050	65	15	600	30

Note: gm/d is grams per day
mg/d is milligrams per day

Old Age

Ageing is universal. Sooner or later everything gets older. But how and when it happens is highly individualised. It also depends on genetic-inheritance, general fitness and one's lifestyle. The essential nutrients and energy-giving food proteins, minerals and vitamins are required in adequate quantities to nourish the body throughout life. The significant change in the diet of ageing persons is that energy nutrients are needed in smaller quantities.

Variations in Energy Requirements as Years go by

Age	Requirement
Middle age	1600–1700 cal
60–70 years	1440–1530 cal
70–80 years	1280–1360 cal

Ageing need not mean debility, but this has a lot to do with the mental health of a person. Positive thinking definitely helps in coping with old age.

In planning diets for aged persons the following aspects need to be carefully considered:

1) Meals should be evenly spaced with smaller amounts of food taken at more frequent intervals.
2) Adjustment of energy intake to achieve the desirable body weight will relieve the strain imposed on arthritic joints, the heart and the body systems.
3) The daily food should consist mainly of milk, meat, egg, wholegrains, vegetables and fruits with a restricted amount of concentrated sweets and fats.

If an old person has a problem chewing these then he can take fresh juices. It is the best alternative. At this age vitamin supplements may be advantageous. Foods should be chosen from the menu according to the individual's tastes and presented in attractive and appetising forms. Many old people have little pleasure in their lives except their meals and they should not be deprived of this.

Pregnancy and Lactation

For pregnant and lactating mothers the diet is of added importance because the mother is nourishing the child through her own body, either in the uterus before birth or through her milk after birth. The nutrients needed for the child should be furnished in the mother's diet. The nutritive needs during pregnancy are best met by a simple wholesome diet rich in proteins, vitamins, minerals, iron and folate. The basis of such a diet is milk products, milk, eggs, meat, legumes, nuts, wholegrains, lentils, soya bean products, leafy vegetables and fruits.

If the diet before pregnancy was adequate then only simple modifications are required to meet all the additional nutrient allowances. The addition of 2 glasses of milk or cheese, one egg, a large amount of fish, poultry or legumes or one serving of green vegetables with frequent substitution of fruit for rich desserts or organ meat is enough.

Table 6.7 : Recommended Dietary Allowance for Pregnant Women

Particulars	*Body wt (kg)*	*Net energy*	*Protein*	*Fat*	*Iron*	*Calcium*
Pregnant Women	50	2100 cal	65 gm/d	25 gm/d	38 mg/d	1000 mg/d

**gm/d – grams per day*

Mg/d – milligrams per day

Diet for Nursing Mothers

During lactation there is an increased need for energy, protein, minerals and vitamins, to constantly replace the amount secreted in the milk of the mother for the nourishment of the infant. The energy requirement varies with the amount of milk produced and therefore, the intake of nourishment must be regulated accordingly.

Table 6.8 : Recommended Dietary Allowance for Lactating Mothers

Particulars Lactation	*Body wt (kg)*	*Net energy*	*Protein*	*Fat*	*Iron*	*Calcium*
0–6 months	50	2,350 cal	75 gm/d	35 gm/d	30 gm/d	1,000 mg/d
6–12 month	50	2,200 cal	68 gm/d	35 gm/d	30 mg/d	1,000 mg/d

**gm/d – grams per day*

Mg/d – milligrams per day

Table 6.9 : Sample Diet for Pregnant Women (3,000 cal)

Time	*Menu*	*Quantity*	*Calories*
Early morning	Fresh lime with sugar		20
	and salt		20
	Light tea with sugar and 3 glucose or wholewheat biscuits		60
Breakfast	Missi roti	2, big size	100
	Curd	150 ml, 1 katori	50
	Apple	1	70
Mid-morning	Wholemilk with Bournvita	1 glass	240
	Biscuits	2	80
Lunch	Black gram soup with cream	1 cup	100
	Chicken curry	25 gm	200
	Spinach with dal	100 gm, 40 gm	250
	Rice and chapatis	20 gm, 2 medium	210
	Curd	1 katori	150
	Raw salad	as desired	-
	Fresh fruit mix (sapota, banana, grapes, orange)	1 cup	200
Evening	Sprouts with lemon	40 gm	150
	Fruit juice	1 glass	120
Dinner	Chicken soup	1 cup	170
	Fried potatoes	1 serving	240

Time	*Menu*	*Quantity*	*Calories*
	Mixed vegetables	1 serving	200
	Baked vegetable pie	1cup	200
	Buns		140
	Caramel custard	1 serving	140
Bedtime	Milk	1 glass	120
	Total		3,230

Table 6.10 : Sample Diet for Lactating Mothers (2800 cal)

Time	*Menu*	*Quantity*	*Calories*
Early morning	Tea with biscuit	2	40
Breakfast	Missi paranthas	2	240
	Curd	1 cup	120
	Papaya	100 gm	100
Mid-morning	Milk	1 glass	120
	Sprouts	40 gm	100
Lunch	Chapatis	2, medium	140
	Rice	25 gm	80
	Palak paneer	1 serving	220
	Dal	1 serving	180
	Curd with cucumber	1 cup	120
	Watermelon or seasoned fruit	as desired	120
Snacks	Colocasia roll	2	220
	Lassi	1 glass	120
Dinner	Chicken/vegetable soup	1 cup	100
	Mixed vegetables with cheese	1 serving	100
	Dal with spinach	1 serving	250
	Curd	1 cup	150
	Rice	25 gm	80
	Chapatis	2, medium	140
	Ice cream	1 serving	110
	Total		2, 850

Special Diets

Nutritional requirements for abnormal physiological conditions must be formulated as a special diet. Undesirable foods from meals have to be omitted and the patient must change his eating habits for life, if he has to follow the special diets for a long period of time.

Low-Sodium Diets

Sodium or salt has an active role in maintaining body fluid pH and body fluid volume. Under conditions like nephritis, cardiac diseases, cirrhosis of the liver, toxemia in pregnancy and hypertension, the sodium concentration increases, resulting in fluid retention or oedema in the body. In these conditions, the most successful treatment for prevention of further oedema is the restriction of sodium content in the diet. The salt or sodium content should be restricted according to the severity of the disease and oedema using the following guidelines:

Mild Restriction

In the case of mild heart damage, the sodium intake should be restricted to 2–3 gm a day. Deletion of highly salted foods from the diet is sufficient to achieve this level.

Moderate Restriction

If the patient has oedema, the sodium intake should be restricted to about 1 gm a day. To achieve this level, it is necessary to omit salt (sodium chloride) completely from the diet and permit foods which are low or moderate in sodium.

Severe Restriction

In the case of cognitive heart disease or failure, severe oedema and hypertension, the sodium intake should be restricted to about 0.5–0.3 gm a day. This level is difficult to achieve and therefore it is necessary that only foods low in sodium be permitted.

Table 6.11 : Guidance on Food Selection

Type of food	*Restriction*	*Amount*	*Foods to be Included*	*Foods to be excluded*
Milk	Severe Moderate Mild	2 cups 3 cups 3 cups	Evaporated non-fat dry milk, unsalted buttermilk and wholemilk	Seasoned buttermilk, condensed milk, whole milk drinks prepared with malt, chocolate syrup and ice cream
Other Beverages	Severe Moderate Mild	2–3 cups As desired -do-	Cocoa prepared with milk allowance: coffee, instant and regular carbonated beverages limited to one 8-oz (250 ml) bottle/day	Fountain beverages, instant cocoa, alcoholic beverages allowed with physician's permission
Soup		1 cup (250 ml)	Unsalted broth, unsalted vegetable soup, made with vegetable having low sodium content, unsalted cream soup made from butter, and milk or unsalted tomato soup.	All canned dehydrated and frozen soups containing salt, consomme and other commercial soups

Type of food	*Restriction*	*Amount*	*Foods to be Included*	*Foods to be excluded*
Meat, poultry, fish	Severe Moderate Mild	110 gm 275 gm 160 gm	Fresh, unsalted, frozen or unsalted canned meats, fish and poultry such as beef, chicken, duck, lamb, pork fresh turkey and fresh fish only	All salted, koshered, smoked and canned meat fish and poultry, chipped or corned beef, ham, frankfurters, caviar, sardines, crabs, lobsters and shrimps
Cheese		1 serving 25 gm	Unsalted cottage cheese, unsalted cream cheese (Mild-American, Cheddar, Swiss, cottage, cream)	All other kinds of cheese not listed as allowed
Eggs	Severe Moderate Mild	1 / day 2/day 2/day	Boiled, poached, scrambled or fried in unsalted butter	None except in excess of amount allowed
Potato or substitutes		2 servings (½ cup per serving)	Potatoes white or sweet, macaroni, noodles, rice and spaghetti	Potato chips and prepared potato products

Type of food	*Restriction*	*Amount*	*Foods to be Included*	*Foods to be excluded*
Bread	Severe Moderate Mild	4 servings 6 servings 4 servings	Unsalted bread and unsalted crackers Regular bread, biscuits and muffins	Regular bread, biscuit rolls, muffins and cereal products prepared with salt or baking soda
Cereals	Severe Moderate Mild	(½cup serving) 1 serving (½ cup per serving)	Unsalted slow-cooked unenriched cereals, barley cornmeal, cornstarch, tapioca dry cereals, puffed rice, puffed and shredded wheat, semolina and sago	Commercial mixes, crackers Quick cooking and enriched cereals, dry cereals except those listed as allowed
Vegetables	Severe Moderate Mild	3 servings -do- 4 servings (½ cup per serving)	All fresh or frozen and unsalted canned vegetables except those listed under foods excluded, dried lima beans, lentils, split peas and soya beans	Canned vegetables and vegetable juices to which salt has been added, beets, carrots, spinach, mustard greens, frozen vegetables Processed with salt, fenugreek and amaranth
Fruit and fruit juice	Severe Moderate	3 servings	Any fruit or fruit juice, fresh frozen or canned except those listed under foods to be excluded, include one citrus fruit or juice daily	Tomato juice, all fruits to which sodium colouring, sodium flavouring or sodium benzoate has been added

Type of food	*Restriction*	*Amount*	*Foods to be Included*	*Foods to be excluded*
Butter or fat	Severe Moderate Mild	6 servings (1 tsp per serving)	Unsalted butter, unsalted margarine unsalted salad and cooking fats such as corn, cottonseed olive oil, unsalted French and mayonnaise dressings, unsalted gravy, sweet and sour cream (limited to 2 tbsps per day)	Salted butter and salted margarine, all commercial salad and mayonnaise dressings, bacon and pork, fat and salted meat gravy
Dessert		As desired	Fruit ice, gelatin prepared with fruit juices, desserts made from milk and egg allowances such as custard, cornstarch and rice pudding, unsalted fruit crisps, fruit pies and sugar cookies	All commercial cakes, cookies, pies, puddings and all deserts, made with baking powder, salt, soda and nuts
Sweets		As desired	cake, cookies, pies, Sugar, white and brown, honey, jams, jellies made without	Commercial candies and syrups, chocolate syrups, and sucaryl

Type of food	Restriction	Amount	Foods to be Included	Foods to be excluded
			the addition of sodium benzoate, hard candy, maple syrup and gum drops	
Spices		As desired	All except those listed in foods to be excluded	Dried or fresh celery leaves, celery salts, celery seeds, garlic salts, salt substitute unless recommended by a physician, all seasonings with salt added
Miscellaneous		As desired	Low sodium dietetic meat extracts and tenderizers, yeast, unsalted popcorn, sodium-free baking powder if allowed by the physician	Chilli sauce, meat extracts, meat tenderizers, meat sauces, mustard sauce, olives pickles, soya sauce, salted popcorn, salted nuts, chips and all snacks containing salt

Note: Supplementation with iron and thiamine may be necessary in strict sodium regimens.

General Rules

1) Avoid the use of salt, baking soda or baking powder in cooking or for table use.
2) Avoid medicines, laxatives and salt substitutes unless prescribed by the physician.
3) Read labels of packaged foods carefully for sodium or salt content.

Guidance for selecting foods low in sodium keeping in mind the restrictions imposed, is given in the following table:

Weight-Reduction Diets

Being overweight or obesity is an abnormal physiological condition. It places considerable strain on the body and often leads to other complications such as diabetes mellitus, cardiovascular diseases and other illnesses. Weight reduction is also important in the treatment of gall bladder, gout and renal diseases. Low calorie foods designed for weight reduction may be formulated by using artificial sweeteners instead of sugar, consuming high and low fat foods.

Table 6.12 : Foods Allowed and Foods Forbidden in a Weight-Reduction Diet

Food Allowed	*Amount*	*Food Not Allowed*
Meat and Fish Group	75–100 gm twice	
Lean roast meat	a day	Pork
Chicken		Bacon
Turkey		Goose
Lean fish		Duck
Shellfish prepared without fat		Fat fish (Tuna and Salmon)
Dairy and Egg group		
Egg, boiled or poached	1 a day	Wholemilk
		Cream
Milk (skimmed or buttermilk)	300 ml	Butter
Cottage cheese (dry)	100 gm daily	Cheese other than cottage cheese

Vegetable and Fruit Group		
Vegetables unlimited except those mentioned in foods not allowed		Potato, yam, sweet potato, colocasia
Fresh fruits in moderation		
Bread and Cereal Group		
Bread (enriched or whole wheat)	1 slice daily	Cakes, pastries
Miscellaneous		
Spices and in moderation condiments		Gravy
Lemon	Unlimited	Sauces
Vinegar	Unlimited	Dressings
Artificial sweetner	As needed	Olives
Tea/coffee	for sweetening	Pickles
Clear broth or bouillon	Substantial proportions	Nuts and nut butter
		Carbonated and alcoholic beverages

Special Instructions

1) Eat only small portions of allowed foods. For example 110 ml of orange juice = 50 cal; 220 ml = 100 cal (calorically equal to cola drinks).
2) Avoid all kinds of trimmings. Mayonnaise, standard salad dressings, all kinds of gravy and sauces, for example, are all very high in calories, frequently higher than the foods they are eaten with.
3) No in-between meal snacks. If unavoidable, due to excessive hunger, snacks should consist of fresh, raw vegetables such as tomatoes, cucumbers, lettuce, carrots and celery. These are all very low in calories and all require chewing.

The treatment of obesity involves both patience and physician motivation. Although the diet remains the core of any treatment regimen, an exercise programme should be combined with the diet. Together they make an ideal pair for preventing and treating obesity. It takes far too much activity to burn up calories and consequently, to achieve a significant weight loss. For example, it takes as many as 35 miles to walk off only one pound. That means a brisk walk for a mile everyday can prevent the gain of a pound every 35 days or more than 10 pounds in a year. Therefore, exercise as part of one's lifestyle is useful to prevent weight gain and to maintain weight loss.

Low-Fat Diet

Low fat foods are recommended for gall bladder and colic diseases. As fat is the most concentrated form of energy, low fat foods are a must in the battle against obesity. A number of products with low fat contents are commercially available. A typical low calorie, low fat diet includes cornflakes, porridge, rava idli mix, dhokla mix, etc. It is heartening to note that with the availability of products such as fat-free milk, cholesterol-free eggs, polyunsaturated low-calorie butter and brown bread, dieting has become an easier task for an average diet-conscious person.

Table 6.13 : Selecting Foods for a Low-Fat (30 gm) Diet

Food allowed in a Low Fat Diet	*Food to be avoided*
1. Skimmed milk, buttermilk and yogurt made from skimmed milk	1. Cream and whole milk
2. Cottage cheese	2. Cheese except uncreamed cottage cheese
3. Egg in life (but limited in number)	3. Egg yolk high in cholesterol
4. Butter and margarine — usually 1 tbsp daily	4. All fats except a very small amount of butter or margarine
5. Very lean fish, fowl and meats — limited fat-free soup broth	5. Fatty meats such as pork, ham bacon, goose, duck and fatty fish
6. Cooked vegetables, lettuce, tomatoes, fruit juice, bananas, citrus fruits without membranes	6. Commercially prepared soups or any soups made with whole milk or cream
7. Refined bread and cereals	7. Salad dressings, gravies
8. Gelatin, angel cake, cereal pudding made of skim milk	8. Desserts except for those on the allowed list
9. Coffee, tea, carbonated beverages, jelly, honey	9. Chocolate, nuts, coconut fried foods, garlic, pickles

Table 6.14 : Sample Menu for a Low-Fat Diet

Breakfast	*Lunch*	*Dinner*
Orange juice	Tomato juice	1 cup dal
Rice flakes with 1 tbsp sugar and 1 cup skim milk	Uncreamed cottage cheese on fruit Salad	Boiled potato with spinach
1 slice toast	2 slices toast with 2 tbsp honey	Raw vegetable salad
1 tbsp jelly	Angel cake	1 chapati
Coffee	1 cup milk/tea	1 tbsp jelly
		Seasoned fruit
		1 cup milk/tea

Soft Diet

A soft diet is very similar to the regular diet except that the texture of the food is modified. It may be ordered for postoperative (after surgery) cases, for patients with severe gastrointestinal conditions or chewing problems. The foods allowed in a soft diet are those which contain very little indigestible carbohydrates and no tough connective tissues. Meat in a soft diet is very tender and may be ground or minced. Most fruits must be cooked, but bananas, oranges, grapes, sapota (with membrane removed) are sometimes allowed. Usually fresh tender cooked vegetables are served, though in a pureed form. Generally, the soft diet foods are mildly flavoured, slightly seasoned or unseasoned and are prepared in an easily digestible form.

Table 6.15 : Selecting Soft Diet Food

Foods to be included	*Foods to be Avoided*
Milk, cream, butter	Meat and shellfish with tough connective tissues
Mild cheese such as cottage or cream cheese	
Eggs except fried	Coarse cereals
Tender chicken, fish, sweetbreads, ground beef, lamb	Condiments
Soup broth and strained cream soups	Rich pastries and desserts
Tender cooked vegetables or pureed vegetables	Foods high in cellulose
Fruit juices, cooked fruits	Fried foods
Refined cereals, cooked cereals, spaghetti, noodles	Nuts and coconut
macaroni, enriched white bread	Raw vegetables and raw fruits except those included in foods allowed
Tea, coffee, carbonated beverages	
Sherbet, ices, plain ice cream, custard, puddings, gelatin, plain cookies, angel and sponge cakes	
Salt and some spices	

Table 6.16 : Sample Menu for a Soft Diet

Breakfast	*Lunch*	*Dinner*
Orange juice	Apple juice	Cream of tomato soup
Cream of rice with milk and sugar/ phirni	Creamed chicken with peas and noodles	Plain lentils
		Mashed potatoes with butter
Buttered toast	Bread and butter or chapatis	Green beans
Tea or coffee with cream and sugar		Bread and butter or chapatis with ghee
	Custard	
	Tea with cream and sugar	Stewed apple
		Milk

High-Fibre Diets

Nutritional Care

An adequate normal diet is followed for patients with constipation, except that it is high in fibre. The diet should include enough bulk (vegetables, fruits, wholegrain cereal products, etc. –Bran, the most concentrated source of food fibre, should be used in moderation.

Table 6.17 : High-Fibre Diet

Fruits (3–5 servings daily)		*Vegetables* (4 servings daily)		*Cereals* (1 serving daily)
Apple	Grapefruit	Asparagus	Lettuce	
Apricots	Peaches	Broccoli	Greens	Oatmeal
Bananas	Pears	Brussels sprout		Shredded wheat
Berries	Pineapple	Carrots	Green beans	Wholewheat cereal
Cherries	Plums	Cabbage	Lima beans	Bran cereal
Figs	Prunes	Cauliflower	Mushrooms	Puffed wheat
Oranges	Dried fruit	Celery	Lady's finger	Bran (2 tbsps daily)
		Corn	Onions	
		Radish	Peas	
		Spinach	Peppers	
		Squash	Potatoes	
		Tomatoes	Turnips	

Soups as desired	*Protein* (3 servings daily)	*Bread* (3–5 servings daily)
Hearty varieties such as vegetable, chowder, bean, tomato, etc.	Fish, meat, egg, chicken, soya beans, etc.	100% whole wheat bread Bread made with coarse ground meal

Desserts (as desired)	*Fats* (if desired)	*Beverages*	*Avoid*
Ices and sherbets Fruit (fresh, frozen, canned) Fruit whips	Butter, margarine cream, salad oil, salad dressings	(6–8 glasses daily) Water, milk (2–3 cups) fruit juice, cocoa, tea	White rice, cream of wheat, white bread, pastries, pies, coffee, noodles, macaroni, cakes, ice cream, highly refined cereals

Low-Fibre Diets

Dietary treatment for severe diarrhoea begins with a fast of 24–48 hours to rest the gastrointestinal tract. Besides this, the nutritional care for adults includes replacement of lost fluids and electrolytes by increasing the oral intake of liquids.

The diet generally adopted is one that will leave very little residue in the intestinal tract. A low-fibre diet is ideal for the treatment of diarrhoea.

Table 6.18 : Low-Fibre Diet

Foods	*Foods Allowed*	*Foods Not Allowed*
Potato and substitutes	Potatoes without skin, rice	
Breads and cereals	Enriched white bread or rolls made from finely milled flour, refined cereals, croutons, breadcrumbs, pancakes, biscuits, unhusked pulses, cornbread	All bran, cracked wheat bread and rolls, branflakes shredded wheat Flakes
Fruit	Strained fruit juices	All fruits
Fats	Any fat	None
Combination dishes	Those made with rice (such as phirni) meat, cheese, fish, sago, cornflour	Any food made with vegetables, fruits or other foods not allowed

Food Groups	*Foods Recommended*	*Foods Which May Cause Distress*
Snacks	Plain crackers, potato chips, corn chips	Anything made from foods not allowed
Beverages		
Milk	Any	None
Milk free beverages	Any	None
Soups	Any creamed or broth based soup without vegetables	Soups with vegetables
Animal Proteins		
Meat	Any	None
Poultry	Any	None
Fish	Any	None
Other Proteins		
Dairy Products		Any cheese
	Yogurt made without fruit or seeds, plain curd	Yogurt with seeds or fruit
	Any eggs	
Vegetables	None	All vegetables
Desserts and Sweets	Anything without seeds and fruits	Anything made with cracked
	a, cornstarch	

Bland-Diet

The bland diet is intended to be soothing to the gastrointestinal tract. The foods are clinically non-irritating. This diet is meant for patients suffering from peptic ulcers and other gastrointestinal problems. Bland food is 'mild or soothing', and has little fibre or roughage.

Principles of Nutritional Care for Peptic Ulcer

The patient suffering from peptic ulcer should:

1) Eat three regular meals daily.
2) Eat small meals to avoid stomach distension.
3) Avoid drinking coffee, tea, cola and other caffeine-containing beverages and alcohol.
4) Cut down on or quit smoking cigarettes.
5) Avoid using large amounts of aspirin or other drugs known to damage the stomach lining.

6) Avoid using excessive pepper in the food.
7) Avoid those foods or drinks that cause discomfort.
8) Eat meals in a relaxed atmosphere.
9) Take antacids 1–3 hours after meals and just before bedtime.

Predisposing Factors That Cause Ulcers

a) Faulty dietary habits, excessive smoking, excessive aspirin intake.
b) Excessive drinking of coffee and cola drinks.
c) Physical stress, inadequate sleep and rest.
d) Emotional conflicts, psychological stress, mental strain.

Table 6.19 : Bland Diet Selection

Food Groups	*Foods Recommended*	*Foods Which May Cause Distress*
Milk and milk products (2 or more cups day)	All milk and milk drinks	None
Vegetables (2 or more servings)	All vegetable juices Cooked vegetables and Salads made from allowed foods	Raw vegetables, dried peas and beans, corn, gas-forming vegetables such as broccoli, brussels sprout, cabbage, onions, cauliflower, cucumber, green pepper, turnip, etc.
Fruits (2 or more servings daily)	All fruit juices	All other fresh and dried fruits
	Cooked or canned fruit Grapefruit and orange segments without membrane	Berries and figs
Breads and cereals (4 or more servings daily)	Enriched breads and cereals	Very coarse cereals such as bran Seeds in or on breads, rolls and crackers Bread and bread products made with nuts or dried fruits or any fried bread

Food Groups	*Foods Recommended*	*Foods Which May Cause Distress*
Potatoes or substitutes	Potatoes Enriched rice, barley, noodles, spaghetti, macaroni and other pastas	Potato chips, fried potatoes, fried rice, wild rice
Meats or substitutes (170 gm daily or more)	All lean tender meats, poultry fish and shellfish Eggs, crisp bacon, lean ham mild cheeses Soyabean and other meat substitutes	Highly seasoned, cured or smoked meats, poultry fish such as sardines Strong flavoured cheeses
Fats	Butter or fortified margarine, mayonnaise, all fats and oils	Salad dressings
Soups	Mildly seasoned meat stock and cream soups made with allowed foods	All other soups
Sweets and syrups	Sugar, honey, syrup, jelly, seedless jam, hard candies, plain chocolate candies, molasses marshmallows, cakes cookies, pies puddings, custard, ice cream, sherbet made from allowed foods	All sweets and desserts containing nuts, coconut or fruit that is not allowed Fried pastries such as doughnut
Beverages	Decaffeinated coffee, cocoa, fruit drinks, 99% caffeine free cola and other carbonated beverages, except other cola drinks	Coffee, tea, alcohol and all cola drinks
Miscellaneous	Iodised salt, flavourings Mildly flavoured gravy and sauces Mild herbs and spices	Strongly flavoured seasonings and condiments such as ketchup, pepper, barbeque sauce, chilli garlic, horseradish, mustard, vinegar, olives, pickles, popcorn, nuts and coconut

High-Calorie Diet

High calorie foods are recommended during a prolonged illness which leads to loss of body weight and malnutrition. Hyperthyroidism and high fever cause weight loss because of increased metabolic disorder. It is important to remember that during an illness, the body loses its reserve nutrients. Therefore, high calorie foods should be nutritionally balanced to restore the lost nutrients to the body.

Example of High-Calorie Foods

Egg, meat, poultry, sugar, candy, chocolate, fats and oils.

Table 6.20 : High-Calorie Diet

Breakfast	*Lunch*	*Dinner*
Fruit juice 2 boiled eggs	Chicken soup with noodles Chicken with tomato	Vegetable soup with cream and skimmed milk powder
Whole wheat toast with butter or Missi parantha with curd	Capsicum with cheese Salad with oil dressing Curd, rice, chapatis Carrot halva	Keema kabab Dal fry Mushroom with cabbage Curd, chapatis, rice Pineapple upside-down pudding

High–Protein Diet

A high-protein diet is sometimes recommended for children and adolescents who need extra protein for growth, for women during pregnancy, for patients recovering from surgery and for those with illnesses resulting in protein loss.

Foods Included in a High-protein Diet

Milk : 3–4 cups
Cheese
Eggs
Lean meats, fish and poultry
Vegetables
Fruits
Cereals (wholegrain or enriched) pulses, legumes, soya bean

Table 6.21 : Sample Menu for a High-Protein Diet

Breakfast	*Lunch*	*Dinner*
Orange juice Scrambled eggs	Meat curry	
Bean sprouts Soya milk	French beans with soya bean chunks	Clear chicken soup Roast chicken
Coffee with cream and sugar	Missi roti, curd Raw salad Fresh fruit cup	Baked potato Green peas Custard, milk Bread and butter

Table 6.22 : High-Protein Menus

	Breakfast	*Lunch*	*Dinner*
I.	Tomato or fruit juice, Bean sprouts	Cheeseburgers Pickles	Soya bean curry, peas, tomato Chopped cucumber in curd Ice-cream
II.	Sliced oranges/ apple Boiled eggs Wholewheat toast, 1 slice	Semolina idli Sambhar Coconut chutney	Meat curry Baked beans Green bean salad Sprouts in curd Caramel custard
III.	Grapefruit juice Egg omelette Wholewheat toast with butter Ice-cream	Mixed dal fry Spinach with soya bean chunks Sprouts in curd Green salad	Chicken and mushroom gravy, creamed spinach, carrots, bean salad, French dressing Bengal gram halwa
IV.	Fruit juice Sausage and tomato	Paneer curry Mushroom with capsicum Missi roti Rice Green bean salad Semolina halwa	Chicken soup with noodles Baked chicken Roasted potatoes Peas and onions Pineapple upside-down cake

Low-Protein Diet

A low protein diet may be prescribed in certain liver and kidney conditions. A low-sodium diet may also be prescribed for patients with kidney disease, resulting in double modification. This diet is deficient in protein, minerals, vitamins and sometimes calories.

Table 6.23 : Selecting Foods for a Low-Protein (25 gm) Diet

Foods Allowed	*Foods Not Allowed*
Milk: ½ cup/day	Milk other than the 1/2 cup allowance
Soups: permitted if made from allowed foods	High protein cereals
1 egg	Legumes
Vegetables: any except corn, lima beans, peas	
Fruits: any	Baked products containing eggs and milk
Bread: 1 serving of cereal, bread, potato or potato substitute	Meat, poultry, fish, cheese, etc
Butter, margarine, cooking oils, salad dressings	
Coffee, tea, carbonated beverages	
Fruit ice, plain hard jelly	
Salts, herbs, spices, pickles	

Table 6.24 : Sample Menu for a Low-Protein (25 gm) Diet

Breakfast	*Lunch*	*Dinner*
Orange juice	Apple juice	Thin dal with bottlegourd
Flaked rice with onion	Spinach and potato	
Coriander chutney	Kadhi, rice	Brinjal with tomato
½ cup milk with sugar	Raw salad	Chapatis, rice
Coffee	Fruit cup	Raw salad
	½ cup jelly	

Vegetarian Diet

Living without Meat

It is a different way of life altogether. Recently vegetarianism has become a popular nutritional alternative in our country. Some of the reasons for choosing a vegetarian diet are:

1. Lower in fat, especially saturated fats often linked with heart disease.
2. Generally lower in calories (a high calorie diet is thought to cause premature ageing and degenerative diseases).
3. Less costly than a diet containing meat, fish, poultry, etc.
4. Ecologically sound.
5. Prevents chemicals used on animal farms and drugs such as hormone boosters which are added to animal feeds from entering the food chain.
6. Becoming a vegetarian does not mean just giving up meat, it means a change of attitude towards food.
7. One of the commonest beliefs is that meat is necessary for good health because it offers better quality proteins than vegetarian food. This is not true as plants are perfectly capable of supplying all the necessary proteins, fats and carbohydrates.
8. Just how nutritious a vegetarian diet is depends, like other diets, on how it is planned. Vegetables, fruits, nuts, grains and pulses are the best sources of minerals like calcium and magnesium, vitamins A, C, E and the B complex group. Dairy products supply vitamin D. When you mix together pulses or legumes such as lentils or beans with cereal grains such as wheat, rice or corn, you get an excellent balance of the essential amino acids (proteins).
9. Vegetarians should take a supplement of vitamin B_{12} just to be absolutely sure they are getting enough, provided their day to day diet includes a good quantity of milk, cheese, soya, legumes, lentils, nuts, sprouted seeds and grains. Nutritionists now believe there is little danger of undernourishment for vegetarians.
10. Try to eat half of your foods raw. Fruits, vegetables cut into salad, nuts and sprouted seeds and grains offer the highest levels of naturally balanced vitamins, minerals

and enzymes of any available food. Along with wholegrains, they are an excellent source of bulk. A salad, far from being a boring bowl of limp greens, can become a good protein source, and the delicious focal point of a meal when it is made of a variety of raw vegetables, then sprinkled with nuts, grated cheese or sunflower seeds for protein.

Special Diet for Diabetes Mellitus

Diabetes is a metabolic disorder attributed to a deficiency of insulin or a complete lack of it. The diet is the cornerstone of therapy for diabetic patients. A diabetic diet is calculated on the basis of 30 cal/kg of ideal body weight, using 40 per cent carbohydrate, 40 per cent fat and 20 per cent protein. Diabetic patients are advised to exclude, carbohydrates that can be easily absorbed like sugar, candy, syrups, etc. The use of non-calorie sweeteners are recommended for such patients.

Foods Allowed for Diabetics

Beverages

Tea without sugar
Coffee without sugar
Soda
Fresh lime
Jaljeera
Kanji
Thin lassi (curd 25 ml)
Clear soup

Condiments, Spices and Herbs

Artificial Sweeteners

Saccharin	Sweetex, Sweet 'N' Low
Aspartame	Sugarfree, Equal, Aspasweet, 1 Up

Salads

Cucumber	Tomato
Bottlegourd	Muskmelon
Watermelon	Lettuce
Radish	Radish leaves

Chutneys and *Pickles*

(Without Oil)
Lemon, chilli and ginger
Onion, radish in vinegar
Cucumber relish
Pickled carrot and radish
Pudina chutney

Mouth Fresheners
Betel leaf, aniseed, cardamom

Vegetables Permitted

Cabbage
Spinach
Knol Khol Greens
Fenugreek leaves
Radish Leaves

Salad Vegetables

Lettuce
Capsicum
Radish
Cucumber
Knol Khol

Seasonal Vegetable

Bean sprouts
Karela
Brinjal
Lauki
Onion
Beetroot
Jackfruit
Lady's finger
Papaya Green
Parwal
Broad beans
Cauliflower
Drumstick
French beans
Turnip
Carrot
Tori
Snakegourd
Tinda
Pumpkin

To Be Avoided	*100 cal*
Colocasia	70g
Sweet potato	60g
Potato	70g
Yam *(Suran)*	90g
Plantain green	110g
Yam	65g
Water chestnut	60g

Fruits Permitted

	100 Cal
Citrus	
Orange	150g
Malta	150g
Sweet Lime (*Musambi*)	150g
Kinnu	150g
Grapes	220g
Other/Non-Citrus	
Apple	120g
Litchi	115g
Peach/Guava	150g
Loquat	160g
Pear/Plum	130g
Phalsa	110g
Papaya	220g
Raspberry	110g
Watermelon	450g
Strawberry	130g
Muskmelon	400g
Apricot	140g
Pomegranate	110g
Sapota (*Cheeku*)	150g
Pineapple	150g
Babugosha	150g
Figs	190g

To Be Avoided

	100 cal
Banana	65g
Mango	100g
Custard Apple	70g
Grapes	100g
Sherifa	70g
Grapes, Purple	120g

Foods to Be Avoided — *100 cal*

Poha (Rice flakes) (*Poha/ Chiewra*)	15g + Oil 2g
Rice Boiled	20g
Puffed Rice	
Pulao (Mixed Vegetable Rice)	
(15g + Oil 2g)	20g
Sago porridge	20g
Macaroni (120g + Oil 3g)	
Noodles (Maggie)	20g
Bourbon Biscuits	15g
Orange Cream Biscuits	15g
Nice Biscuits	15g
Sponge Cake	22g
Fruit Cake (dark)	18g
Pound Cake	15g
Chocolate Cake	19g
Dal Vada	20g
Samosa, Small	30g
Namakpara	13g
Matthi/Papadi	13g
Dal Sev /Mixture	13g
Ganthia	13g
Urad Makhani	
Fryums / *Phool Badi* Fried	13g
Tikki (½)	35g
Potato Chips	12g
Finger Chips 3 (3" x ½ x ½")	25g
Sweet Potato	60g
Semolina (*Suji*) Halva	23g
Jalebi	22g
Gulab Jamun	18g
Rasgulla (squeezed)	25g
Patisa	17g
Barfi	18g
Laddoo	18g
Chiki Rice	
Chiki Chana	
Milk, Buffalo's	60ml

Milk, Cow's	100ml
Arbi (Colocasia Chaat)	65g
Cheeku (Sapota)	80g
Banana	65g
Grapes, Green	100g
Grapes, Purple	129g
Dates (Dried)	22g
Figs (Dried)	23g
Apricots	22g
Coconut (dried)	10g
Chilgoza	11g
Pistachio (*Pista*), Salted	11g
Walnuts, Shelled	10g
Groundnut, Roasted / Salted	12g
Almonds, California/Gurbandi	11g
Cashewnuts	12g
Cashewnuts, Fried	11g
Groundnuts, in Shell	18g
Groundnuts, Fried	11g
Coconut, Fresh	15g
Raisins	25g
Sponge Cake	25g
Cottage Cheese (*Paneer*) (Full Cream)	24g
Cheese, Processed	25g

Foods to Be Strictly Avoided

1. **Sugar and Products** 60 cal/15g
   Sugar (jaggery)
   Syrup
   Jam/Marmalade
   Candies
2. **Choco Bar** 200 cal/40g
3. **Pickles with Oil and Sugar**
   Sweet pickle of lemon (*Meetha Nimbu*)
   Sweet pickle of cauliflower and turnip (*Gobi Shalgam Meetha*)
   Indian gooseberry pickle (*Amla Murrabba*)

4. **Heavy/Sweet Sauces**
   Sonth (tamarind–aniseed–jaggery sauce)
   Mayonnaise
   Chocolate Sauce
   Cream Sauce
5. **Beverages**
   Alcoholic

Beer	300 cal/bottle
Whisky/Rum/Gin	132 cal/45ml
Sherbet/Squashes	80 cal/20ml
Pineapple juice (Tinned)	92 cal/170ml
Aerated Drinks	
Campa/Limca	135 cal/300ml
Tripp/Sprint	90 cal/300ml
Cola Drinks	120 cal/300ml
Cola Lite/Diet Cola (can be taken)	40 cal/bottle

6. **Malt Preparations**

Boost	Horlicks
Maltova	Bournvita

Sample Diets for Diabetics

1. ***Sample diet for a 5-year-old, school-going, insulin-dependent boy, with low body-weight (underweight)***

Blood sugar level: fasting	150 mg %,	post-meal: 250 mg%
Modified dietary allowances:	calories	1300 cal
	carbohydrate	220 gms
	protein	57 gms
	fat	40 gms
	(cooking/visible fat 30 gms, hidden fat 10 gms)	

Sample Menu

Time	*Menu*	*Quantity*	*Calories*
Early Morning			
7.30 a.m.	Milk	1 cup, 150 ml	50
	Marie biscuits	3	75
Breakfast	Boiled egg	1	85
	Bread slices (brown)	2, medium	50
Mid-morning			
Short recess in school	Fruit (guava) or grilled fish	1, small or 1 piece	50
Packed Lunch	Bengal gram and fenugreek roti	2, small	140
	Apple	1, medium	75
Evening			
5 p.m.	Milk	150 ml, 1 cup	85
	Spongy delight	20 gms	150
Dinner			
8 p.m.	Tomato soup	150 ml, 1 cup	50
	Rice 15 gms		50
	Dal 30 gms		155
	French beans vegetable	150 gms	115
	Chapati	15 gm; 1, small	50
Bedtime	Fruit summer cloud	1 serving	100

Note:

1. Use of artificial sweetener should be restricted.
2. Raw salad without oil dressings may be taken as desired.

2. *Sample diet for a 45-year-old diabetic woman*

Blood sugar level:		post-meal 160 mg%
Increased cholesterol:		305 mg%
Build: Medium		
Modified dietary allowances:	calories	1200 cal
	carbohydrate	280 gms
	protein	60 gms
	fat	35 gms (cooking/ visible fat 20 gms, hidden fat 15 gms)

Sample Menu

Time	*Menu*	*Quantity*	*Calories*
Early Morning			
7 a.m.	Tea/coffee with sugar	150 ml, 1 cup	20
Breakfast			
8 a.m.	Skimmed milk with	150 ml, 1 cup	50
	cornflakes	30 gms, 1 cup	100
Mid-morning			
11 a.m.	Marie biscuits/wheat Bran biscuits	2	50
	Apple	1, small	50
Packed Lunch	Sprouted green gram	45 gms, 1 ½ cups	
	Chapatis 3, medium	60 gms	210
	Salad		
Evening			
4.30 p.m.	Tea/coffee without sugar	150 ml, 1 cup	20
Dinner			
8.30 p.m.	Tomato and cauliflower	200 gms, 1 cup	150
	Black gram dal	20 gms, 1 cup	130
	Plain rice	15 gms, ½ cup	50
	Chapatis	40 gms 2, medium	
	Salad		140

Note:

1. *Artificial sweetener may be used.*
2. *Skimmed milk and its products to be used.*
3. *Raw salad without oil dressing may be taken as much as desired.*

UNIT VII

READY RECKONERS

Check Your Weight

Height and Weight of Children (Average)

Boys					*Girls*			
Height		*Weight*		*Age in*	*Height*		*Weight*	
ins	*cm*	*lb*	*kg*	*years*	*ins*	*cm*	*lb*	*kg*
29.6	75.2	22.2	10.1	1	29.2	74.2	21.5	9.8
34.4	87.5	27.7	12.6	2	34.1	86.6	27.1	12.3
37.9	96.2	32.2	14.6	3	37.7	95.7	31.8	14.4
40.7	103.4	36.4	16.5	4	40.6	103.2	36.2	16.4
43.8	111.3	42.8	19.4	5	43.2	109.7	41.4	18.8
46.3	117.5	48.3	21.9	6	45.6	115.9	46.5	21.1
48.9	124.1	54.1	24.5	7	48.1	122.3	52.2	23.7
51.2	130.0	60.1	27.3	8	50.4	128.0	58.1	26.3
53.3	135.5	66.0	29.9	9	52.3	132.9	63.8	28.9
55.2	140.3	71.9	32.6	10	54.6	138.6	70.3	31.9
56.8	144.2	77.6	35.2	11	57.0	144.7	78.8	35.7
58.9	149.6	84.4	38.3	12	59.8	151.9	87.6	39.7
61.0	155.0	93.0	42.2	13	61.9	157.1	99.1	44.9
64.1	162.7	107.6	48.8	14	62.8	159.6	108.4	49.2
66.1	167.8	120.1	54.5	15	63.4	161.1	113.4	51.5
67.6	171.6	129.7	58.8	16	63.9	162.2	117.0	53.1

Source: Treasure Home Medical Handbook, Sun Publication

Weight of Adults (Average)

Men

Average Weight in Pounds and Kilograms (in Indoor Clothing)

Height (with shoes)

			17–19 Yrs		*20–24 Yrs*	
ft	*in*	*cm*	*lb*	*kg*	*lb*	*kg*
5	2	157.5	119	54.0	128	58.1
5	3	160.0	123	55.8	132	59.9
5	4	162.6	127	57.6	136	61.7
5	5	165.1	131	59.4	139	63.0
5	6	167.6	135	61.2	142	64.4
5	7	170.2	139	63.0	145	65.8
5	8	172.7	143	64.9	149	67.6
5	9	175.3	147	66.7	153	69.4
5	10	177.8	151	68.5	157	71.2
5	11	180.3	155	70.3	161	73.0
6	0	182.9	160	72.6	166	75.3
6	1	185.4	164	74.2	170	77.1
6	2	188.0	168	76.2	174	78.9
6	3	190.5	172	78.0	178	80.8
6	4	193.0	176	79.8	181	82.5

		25–29 Yrs		*30–39 Yrs*		*40–49 Yrs*	
ft	*in*	*lb*	*kg*	*lb*	*kg*	*lb*	*kg*
5	2	134	60.8	137	62.1	140	63.5
5	3	138	62.6	141	64.0	144	65.3
5	4	141	64.0	145	65.8	148	67.1
5	5	144	65.3	149	67.6	152	68.9
5	6	148	67.1	153	69.4	156	70.8
5	7	151	68.5	157	71.2	161	73.0
5	8	155	70.3	161	73.0	165	74.8
5	9	159	72.1	165	74.8	169	76.7
5	10	163	73.9	170	77.1	174	78.9
5	11	167	75.8	174	78.9	178	80.0
6	0	172	78.0	179	81.2	183	83.0
6	1	177	80.3	183	83.0	187	84.8
6	2	182	82.6	188	85.3	192	87.1
6	3	185	84.4	193	87.5	197	89.4
6	4	190	86.2	199	90.3	203	92.1

Women

Average Weight in Pounds and Kilograms (in Indoor Clothing)

Height (with shoes)

			17–19 Yrs		20–24 Yrs	
ft	*ins*	*cm*	*lb*	*kg*	*lb*	*kg*
4	10	147.3	99	44.9	102	46.3
4	11	149.9	102	46.6	105	47.6
5	0	152.2	105	47.6	108	49.0
5	1	154.9	109	49.4	112	50.8
5	2	157.5	113	51.3	115	52.2
5	3	160.0	116	52.6	118	53.5
5	4	162.6	120	54.4	121	54.9
5	5	165.1	124	56.2	125	56.7
5	6	167.6	127	57.6	129	58.5
5	7	170.2	130	59.0	132	59.9
5	8	172.7	134	60.8	136	61.7
5	9	175.3	138	62.6	140	63.5
5	10	177.8	142	64.4	144	65.3
5	11	180.3	147	66.7	149	67.6
6	0	182.9	152	69.9	154	69.9

		25–29 Yrs		30–39 Yrs		40–49 Yrs	
ft	*ins*	*lb*	*kg*	*lb*	*kg*	*lb*	*kg*
4	10	107	48.5	115	52.2	122	55.7
4	11	110	49.9	117	53.1	124	56.2
5	0	113	51.3	120	54.4	127	57.6
5	1	116	52.6	123	55.8	130	59.0
5	2	119	54.0	126	57.2	133	60.3
5	3	122	55.3	129	58.5	136	61.7
5	4	125	56.7	132	59.9	140	63.5
5	5	129	58.5	135	61.2	143	64.9
5	6	133	60.3	139	63.0	147	66.7
5	7	136	61.7	142	64.4	151	68.5
5	8	140	63.5	146	66.2	155	70.3
5	9	144	65.3	150	68.0	159	72.1
5	10	148	67.1	154	69.9	164	74.4
5	11	153	69.4	159	72.5	169	76.7
5	12	158	71.7	164	74.4	174	78.9

GRADES OF EXERCISE VIS-Á-VIS CALORIE CONSUMPTION

Exertion Grade	*Calorie/Minute*
Mild or light (walking, sweeping floor)	1.9
Moderate (brisk walking, slow horseback riding, golf, washing clothes)	3.1
Heavy (running, swimming, tennis)	5.4

Calories Burnt during Physical Activity

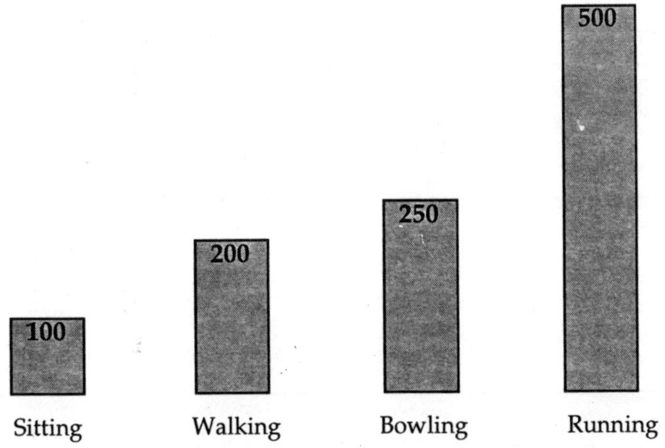

Physical exercise plays an important part in weight control and weight loss. The more physically active you are, the greater the number of calories burned, as shown here for an average woman five feet five inches tall and weighing 130 pounds. The numbers refer to the number of calories burned per hour.

WORDS OF WISDOM FOR DIETERS

Here is the collected, distilled wisdom of behavioural scientists and generations of dieters for sticking to your decision to lose weight. Pick and choose to meet your individual needs.

a) Exercise instead of eating. Jog, dance or go for a walk.
b) Remove 'extra' food from your environment. Keep only enough diet food for a day on hand.
c) When you feel like eating, grab a carrot or a piece of celery.

d) Relax. Learn exercises that remove tension and stress, and perform them when you feel like eating.
e) Eat slowly. Be conscious of the texture, smell and taste of what you eat.
f) Keep a detailed daily diary of what you eat, when you eat, and how you feel about it.
g) Count calories.
h) Do not skip breakfast.
i) Weigh yourself every morning.
j) Buy clothing a size smaller and keep it on a visible spot.

Table 7.1 : Maximum Calories a Day

Women

To Maintain This weight kgs	*Age 18–35*	*Age 35–55*	*Age 55–75*
	Daily intake of calories	*Daily intake of calories*	*Daily intake of calories*
47	1700	1500	1300
49	1850	1650	1400
54	2000	1750	1550
59	2125	1925	1625
65	2300	2050	1800
70	2500	2250	2000

Men

To Maintain This Weight kgs	*Age 18–35*	*Age 35–55*	*Age 55–75*
	Daily intake of calories	*Daily intake of calories*	*Daily intake of calories*
49.9	2200	1950	1700
55.0	2400	2150	1900
59.4	2525	2275	2026
63.5	2700	2400	2250
71.0	2800	2600	2400
74.8	3100	2800	2650
78.9	3250	3000	2850
83.5	3400	3200	3000

Personal Weight Chart

Record your weight once a week in the chart on this page. Then, plot your weight on the graph so that you can visualise your progress more easily.

Date	WT In lbs	Weight in lbs													
		300													
		275													
		250													
		225													
		200													
		195													
		190													
		185													
		180													
		175													
		170													
		165													
		160													
		155													
		150													
		145													
		140													
		135													
		130													
		125													
		120													
		115													
		110													
		105													
		100													
			0	1	2	3	4	5	6	7	8	9	10	11	12

No. of Weeks on Diet

For example, a man weighing 180 lbs took Sterling's 30-day diet to lose weight. He took the diet for 60 days, ie 8 weeks. He lost 5 lbs after three weeks, another 4/5 lbs in the next three weeks and an additional 2 lbs in the last two weeks. When plotted on the personal weight chart, the graph will show as follows:

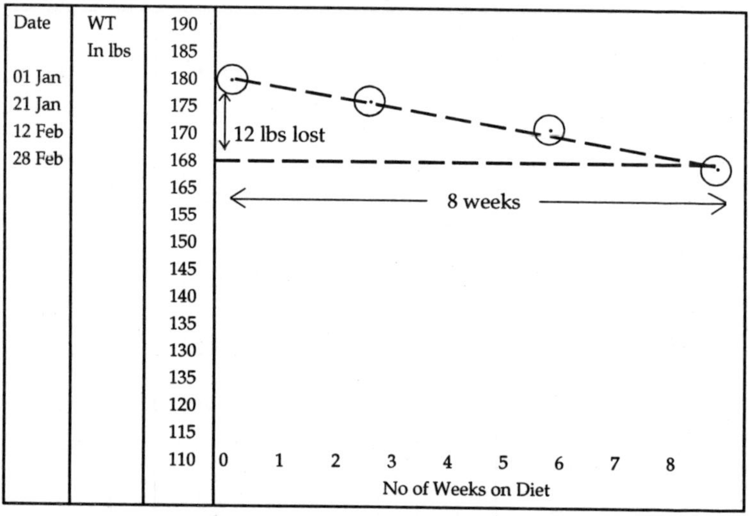

High Cholesterol Foods

- Beef
- Pork
- Lamb
- Veal
- Mackerel
- Salmon
- Sturgeon
- Trout
- Crab
- Lobster
- Kidneys
- Oyster
- Sausages
- Liver
- Sweetbread
- Heart and Brain
- Giblets
- Tongue
- Egg yolk
- Butter
- Cream
- Caviar
- Cheese
- Condensed milk
- Whole milk and its products

Table 7.2 : Nutritive Value of Soya milk (as Compared with Animal Milk)

	Soya milk	*Animal milk*
1.	276 ml gives 100 calories	166 ml gives 100 calories
2.	Protein 8.6 gms	5.3 gms
3.	Fat (unsaturated) 4.9 gms	5.1 gms (saturated)
4.	Carbohydrates 4.9 gms	8.3 gms
5.	Dietary fibre 4.5 gms	Nil
6.	Iron 4.9 gms	Nil

Though soya milk is as nutritious as the animal milk, it is better suited for diabetic and heart patients.

Energy Provided by Nutrients

There are three basic nutrients in food, which provide energy to the body. These include:

Nutrients / gm	*Energy in calories*
Carbohydrate	4
Fat	9
Protein	4

Table 7.3 : Calorie Content of Beverages

Beverage	*Measure*	*Calories*
1. Tea		
Tea without sugar, skimmed milk	150 ml, 1 cup	5
Tea with 1 teaspoon sugar and cow's milk	150 ml, 1 cup	20
2. Coffee*		
Coffee without skimmed milk	150 ml, 1 cup	9
Coffee with 1 teaspoon sugar and cow's milk	150 ml, 1 cup	35

---

* *Caffeine in coffee is a very powerful stimulant. It should not be given to children. These drinks are rich in calories and are rapidly absorbed by the tissues leading to rapid rise in blood sugar. They have poor nutritive value and should be avoided.*

3. **Cocoa**		
Cocoa, without sugar, with skimmed milk	150 ml, 1 cup	10
Cocoa, with a teaspoon of sugar and cow's milk	150 ml, 1 cup	35
4. **Bournvita**		
Skimmed milk with a teaspoon of Bournvita	150 ml, 1 cup	70
Cow's milk with one teaspoon of Bournvita and 1 teaspoon sugar	150 ml, 1 cup	140

Note: A teaspoon of Bournvita contains 18.5 calories.

5. **Buttermilk** (made of 1 glass skimmed milk curd)	220 ml	37
6. **Aerated Water****		
Soda with fresh lime/Jaljeera	1 glass, 220 ml	nil
7. **Coconut Water**	1 cup, 150 ml	25.5

8. Alcoholic Beverages

Item	*Measure*		*Calories*
Beer	1 glass	250 ml	98
Whisky	1 peg	60 ml	162
Rum	1 peg	60 ml	162
Toddy (fermented)	1 glass	240 ml	24
Gin	1 peg	60 ml	162

***Aerated water is carbonated water stored in sealed bottles. It is also called soda water. It helps in relieving indigestion.*

Calorie Check

Table 7.4 : Calorie Reckoner, A Concise Chart to Get You Started

All the Values are per 100 gms of Edible Portion

Name of the Foodstuff	Calories
Cereals, Grains and Products	
Millet	361
Maize	342
Rice	349
Rice Bran	393
Riceflakes	346
Rice, Puffed	325
Wheat flour, whole	341
Wheat flour, refined	348
Wheat semolina	348
Wheat vermicelli	352
Wheat bread, brown	244
Wheat bread, white	245
Pulses and Legumes	
Bengal gram, whole	360
Bengal gram dal	372
Bengal gram, roasted	369
Black gram dal	347
Green gram, whole	334
Green gram, whole	348
Horse gram, whole	321
Khesari dal	345
Lentils	343
Moth beans	330
Peas, green	93
Peas, dry	315
Peas, roasted	340
Rajmah	346
Red gram dal	335
Red gram tender	116
Soyabean	432

Name of the Foodstuff	Calories
Leafy Vegetables	
Amaranth	45
Bathua leaves	30
Bengal gram leaves	97
Bottlegourd leaves	39
Brussels sprouts	52
Cabbage	27
Carrot leaves	77
Cauliflower greens	66
Celery Leaves	37
Colocasia leaves	77
Coriander leaves	44
Fenugreek leaves	49
Mint	48
Mustard leaves	34
Spinach	26
Roots and Tubers	
Carrot	48
Colocasia	97
Onion, big	50
Onion, small	59
Parsnip	101
Potato	97
Radish, pink	32
Sweet potato	120
Tapioca	157
Turnip	29
Yam, ordinary	111
Other Vegetables	
Beans scarlet runner	158
Bittergourd	25

Name of the Foodstuff	*Calories*
Bittergourd, small	60
Bottlegourd	12
Brinjal	24
Broad beans	48
Cauliflower	30
Cluster beans	16
Cucumber	13
Double beans	85
Drumstick	26
French beans	26
Capsicum	24
Jackfruit, tender	51
Jackfruit seeds	133
Khol-khol	21
Lady's fingers	35
Lotus stem, dry	234
Mango, green	44
Papaya	27
Ridgegourd	17
Snakegourd	18
Tinda	21
Tomato	23
Nuts and Oilseeds	
Almond	655
Cashewnut	596
Chilgoza	615
Coconut, dry	662
Coconut, fresh	444
Coconut milk	430
Coconut water	24
Coconut meal	312
Coconut, tender	41
Groundnut	567
Groundnut, roasted	570
Linseeds	530
Mustard seeds	541
Pistachio nuts	626
Safflower seeds	356
Sunflower seeds	620
Walnut	687

Name of the Foodstuff	*Calories*
Condiments and Spices	
Asafoetida	297
Cardamom	229
Chillies, dry	246
Cloves, dry	286
Coriander	288
Cumin seeds	356
Fenugreek seeds	333
Garlic, dry	145
Ginger, fresh	67
Mango powder	337
Nutmeg	472
Poppy seeds	408
Tamarind pulp	283
Turmeric	349
Fruits	
Amla	58
Apple	59
Apricot	53
Apricot, dry	306
Banana	116
Cashew fruit	51
Cherries, red	64
Dates, dry	317
Dates, fresh	144
Figs	37
Grapes, green	71
Grapes, purple	58
Grapes, seedless	45
Grapefruit triumph	32
Guava	
Jackfruit	88
Jambu fruit	62
Lemon, sweet	35
Lemon	57
Litchi	61
Lime	59
Lime, sweet malta	36
Lime, sweet mausambi	43
Loquat	43
Mahua, ripe	111

Name of the Foodstuff	*Calories*
Mango, ripe	74
Melon, musk	17
Watermelon	16
Mulberry	49
Orange juice	9
Papaya, ripe	32
Peaches	50
Pears	52
Pineapple	46
Plum	52
Pomegranate	65
Raspberry	56
Sapota	98
Tomato, ripe	20
Fishes and Other Seafood	
Chela	103
Chingri, small, dried	292
Crab muscle	59
Crab, small	169
Herring, Indian	119
Hilsa	105
Lobster	90
Mackerel	93
Oil sardine	97
Pomfret, black	111
Pomfret, white	87
Prawn	899
Rohu	97
Sardine	97
Shark	101
Shrimp	349
Singhara	167
Meat and Poultry	
Beef	410
Duck	130
Egg, duck	181
Egg, hen	173

Name of the Foodstuff	*Calories*
Fowl	109
Goat, meat	118
Mutton	194
Pork	114
Milk and Milk Products	
Milk, buffalo	117
Milk, cow	67
Milk, goat	72
Milk, human	65
Curd, cow milk	60
Buttermilk	15
Skimmed milk	28
Cottage Cheese, cow's milk	265
Cottage Cheese, buffalo's milk	292
Cheese	348
Khoa, whole buffalo milk	421
Khoa, skimmed buffalo milk	206
Skimmed milk powder	357
Whole milk powder	496
Fats and Edible Oils	
Butter	729
Ghee, cow	900
Ghee, buffalo	900
Hydrogenated oil	900
Cooking oil	900
Sugars	
Sugarcane	398
Honey	319
Jaggery	358
Sago	351
Beverages, Alcoholic	
Toddy, fermented	38
Beverages Non-Alcoholic	
Sugarcane juice	39

Glossary

Cooking Terms

Bake	:	To cook by dry heat in an oven
Beat	:	To introduce air into a mixture in order to make it more fluffy
Blanche	:	To put into boiling water
Blend	:	To combine and mix ingredients to achieve a smooth and uniform consistency
Boil	:	To bubble and vaporise
Broil	:	To grill
Brown	:	To sear the stuff until its outer surface turns golden brown
Chop	:	To cut into tiny pieces with a sharp knife
Deep fry	:	To cook food by immersing deep into hot fat or oil
Dice	:	To cut into small cubes
Dough	:	Flour kneaded and moistened with water or any other liquid like milk
Fat	:	Any cooking medium like ghee, butter or hydrogenated oils
Fry	:	To cook in shallow fat or oil
Garnish	:	To decorate food with portions of edible foodstuffs for the table
Grate	:	To reduce to small pieces by rubbing on a grater
Gravy	:	Juices that exude from meat and vegetables during and after cooking
Grind	:	To reduce to small particles or powder or paste by crushing
Knead	:	To work up moist flour into dough or paste to make it elastic and well-blended
Marinate	:	To steep in wine, oil, herbs, curd or fat
Melt	:	To heat a solid foodstuff until it becomes liquid
Mix	:	To put two or more ingredients together and then stir until the particles combine
Pare	:	To remove the outer skin of fruit or vegetable
Peel	:	To take the skin off, for example, of an orange or a banana
Simmer	:	To cook a liquid gently just below the boiling point; to boil gently
Soak	:	To immerse in water or any other liquid for some time
Stew	:	To cook or simmer slowly for a long time in a covered pan
Strain	:	To separate liquids from solids by passing them through a sieve